D0560509

Listen Up, Honey

Other Books by Thelma Wells

❋ ❋ ❋

Bumblebees Fly Anyway: Defying the
Odds at Work and Home

The Best Devotions of Thelma Wells

God Will Make a Way

What's Going On, Lord?

Girl, Have I Got Good News for You

The Buzz

Listen Up, Honey

Good News for Your Soul

Thelma Wells

W PUBLISHING GROUP
A Division of Thomas Nelson Publishers
Since 1798

www.wpublishinggroup.com

Published by W Publishing Group, a division of Thomas Nelson, Inc., P.O. Box 141000, Nashville, TN 37214.

W Publishing Group books may be purchased in bulk for educational, business, fund-raising, or sales promotional use. For information, please e-mail SpecialMarkets@ThomasNelson.com.

Unless otherwise indicated, Scripture quotations used in this book are from the New King James Version (NKJV®), copyright © 1979, 1980, 1982, Thomas Nelson, Inc., Publishers. Used by permission.

Other Scripture passages are from these sources: The Message (MSG). Copyright © 1993, 1994, 1995, 1996, 2000, 2001, 2002. Used by permission of NavPress Publishing Group. The New American Standard Bible® (NASB). Copyright © 1960, 1962, 1963, 1968, 1971, 1972, 1973, 1975, 1977, 1995 by The Lockman Foundation. Used by permission. The Holy Bible, New International Version (NIV). Copyright © 1973, 1978, 1984, International Bible Society. Used by permission of Zondervan Bible Publishers. The New Century Version (NCV) © 1987, 1988, 1991 by Word Publishing, a division of Thomas Nelson, Inc. All rights reserved. Used by permission. The Holy Bible, New Living Translation (NLT), copyright © 1996 by Tyndale Charitable Trust. Used by permission of Tyndale House Publishers, Wheaton, IL. The King James Version of the Bible (KJV).

Library of Congress Cataloging-in-Publication Data

Wells, Thelma, 1941–
   Listen up, Honey : lessons Granny taught me about living my life, loving the Lord, and leaving a legacy / Thelma Wells.
      p. cm.
   ISBN 10: 0-8499-0045-X
   ISBN 13: 978-0-8499-0045-7
   1. Christian women—Religious life.   I. Title.
BV4527.W438 2006
248.8'43—dc22   2005035033

Printed in the United States of America
06 07 08 09 10 QW 9 8 7 6 5 4

*I*f wealth can be counted in the number of grandchildren one has, I must be pretty rich with ten grands and one great-grand. This book is dedicated to them:

Antony Cox

Vanessa Wells

Alaya Cohen

Alyssa Wells

Bryna Cohen

Kennedy Tennard

McKinley Tennard

Phillip Wells

Ciara Cohen

Marsaille Tennard

Aubriana Cox

And any others to come.

These children are a precious gift from God. I want to do for them what my great-grandmother did for me: instill in them high moral character, respect for authority, a spirit of sharing, and a passionate love of God. I dare not do less.

I want to be their stability when their world seems to spin out of control, their sounding board when nobody else will listen. I want to be there for hugs when they feel sad and when they're celebrating.

I will love them, nurture them, discipline them, and pray for them, and in my kitchen I'll teach them lessons about cooking—and about living.

Because I am their Grammy.

✻ ✻ ✻

Incline your ear, and come to Me.
Hear, and your soul shall live.

—Isaiah 55:3

Contents

Acknowledgments

One of the most powerful factors in writing a book is having someone who can read what you've written and make sure it's grammatically and journalistically correct. With this said, I must thank Sue Ann Jones, who is one of the most super-duper editors I've worked with. Sue Ann, thanks for making sure I've written correctly.

Without a literary agent, it is difficult to know how to handle the business of writing and publishing. I've been blessed to not have to worry about these details because I have one of the best literary agents in the country. David Van Diest, you are a blessing.

Whatever I write needs someone to promote it, someone who believes in me and the work I do. That's where Sabrina O'Malone of WorkingMom.com has been a trusted help for me. With expert experience in marketing, she is a major team player with David and me.

I appreciate the publisher of this book, W Publishing Group, for encouraging me.

Most of all, I thank the Holy Spirit for inspiring me as

I wrote these pages. It was his revelations that caused me to remember experiences and interpret the Scriptures shared in this book.

To God be the glory for the great things he has done!

Raised on Faith, Filled with Food, Blessed by Love

Listen carefully to Me, and eat what is good,
And let your soul delight itself in abundance.

—ISAIAH 55:2

When my friend Shirley dropped by the other day, she sat down at my kitchen table to talk, just like everybody does who comes to visit me. I have six tables in various rooms throughout my house, but the kitchen table is where everyone automatically gathers. That day Shirley sat at the table and said, "Hey, T" (lots of people call me T), "what do you have to eat? I'm hungry."

I shook my head, a little embarrassed, and admitted, "Honey, I'm sorry, but I don't have a thing prepared to eat."

She laughed and told me, "Girl, Mama Harrell would turn over in her grave if she knew you didn't have anything cooked and nothing in your refrigerator! You're not living out her legacy."

I answered, "That's right, baby. I'm working smarter, not harder!"

It's not that I don't cook—not by a long shot. I cook plenty. A little later I'll tell you how I put on some mouthwatering feasts when my family descends on my house on a routine basis. But I don't spend my life in the kitchen, and I've found some shortcuts along the way that make the time I do spend there a whole lot easier than it was when I was growing up in Mama Harrell's kitchen.

Mama Harrell was my great-grandmother—I called her Granny. She and my great-grandfather—he was known as Daddy Harrell—took me to raise when my mother became too ill to take care of me. We were poor and lived in a back-alley apartment, but Granny always found ways to serve three huge meals a day—hearty stuff that stuck to your bones. For breakfast we'd have bacon *and* ham *and* eggs plus toast and jelly and maybe pancakes too. For lunch Granny would serve some kind of meat and vegetables plus salad and bread. Then for dinner she would often fix two kinds of meat, three different vegetables, bread, and salad. We drank iced tea brewed with Granny's homegrown mint. And whenever I remember Granny's delicious homemade dinner rolls dripping with a pat of real butter and her homemade preserves, I'll have what must be similar to an out-of-body experience. Those dinner rolls were the *best*. And on top of all that, there was always something sweet for dessert.

Granny always had plenty of food. It was important to her to be ready to feed anyone who might come by—and lots of friends, neighbors, and relatives did just that. They would eat and eat and eat then finally push back from the table and say, "Oh, Mama, that was *so* good."

Granny always had plenty of faith too. And she shared it just as readily as she did her cooking. It wasn't unusual for Granny and me to be in church every day of the week, either attending a worship service, a Bible study, a women's meeting, or just helping with the cleaning. Granny loved Jesus with every morsel of her mind, body, and soul, and she taught me to love him the same way. She incorporated that love into everything she did, and it flowed out of her and into everyone she came in contact with.

I loved being with Granny, and since she spent most of her time in the kitchen, that's where I was too. As we worked together, I learned a lot about cooking, a lot about life, and a lot about the Lord. I watched what she did—in the kitchen and out in the world—and I listened to what she told me. All my life I've tried to remember and live out the lessons she taught me. And let me just say, some of those lessons I learned the hard way!

Now I'm trying to follow Granny's example and provide my children and grandchildren with the same kind of love-filled, food-flavored, Scripture-stitched memories I had growing up—or even better.

In this book I also want to share with *you* some of the lessons I've learned and some of the experiences I've had. I'll show you some of the ways I'm passing on those lessons to my family and to others around me. I'll also tell you about some of the ways I've decided *not* to follow in Granny's footsteps. For example, I don't *ever* plan to chase a chicken around the backyard and wring its neck to make sure it's fresh enough to feed my family! And I've given up trying to grow my own fresh vegetables, like Granny did. I tried it once or twice, but it turns out you have to remember to water the poor little things, and I never could manage to do that.

Fried Chicken, Granny's Way

Granny sometimes killed her own chickens for frying, but if she bought the chicken, she never bought one that was already cut up. They cost more, and she said that was a waste of money. She washed the chicken thoroughly (sometimes even sprinkling a little baking soda on the chicken and rinsing it off to make sure it was clean). Then she patted it dry and cut it into twelve pieces: two legs, two thighs, two wings, the wishbone cut off the top of the breast, and the neck. Then she cut both the breast and the back into two pieces. And she'd also fry the liver and gizzard.

Next she rubbed the chicken with salt and pepper and a cut clove of garlic. Then she let it sit awhile in the bowl, maybe thirty minutes, "so the seasoning can go through it," she would say.

She would put some flour in a brown paper bag from the grocery store, then she'd drop in the chicken and toss it around to coat it. And while she was doing that, she was melting Crisco shortening (not Crisco oil) in a big cast-iron skillet on the stove. When the melted shortening was just starting to smoke, she would gently drop in the chicken. She would keep the grease pretty hot to brown the chicken on both sides. It takes a while to cook chicken—anywhere from twenty to forty-five minutes, depending on the size of the pieces. Granny would wait until each piece floated to the top of the grease to determine if it was ready. Some pieces, like the neck, cook a lot faster than the breast. So you need to keep a careful eye on it. And you don't want to crowd it in the grease. Usually it would take Granny two or three batches to get the whole chicken cooked. Granny cooked some *major* fried chicken, sister, let me tell you!

Fried Chicken, Mama T's Way

Albertson's take-out. Honey, they make some goooooood fried chicken!

On the other hand, and not trying to brag, I think I may have even improved on Granny's practices in a few areas (although, because they cost a little more, Granny probably wouldn't approve of a single one of the convenience foods I use to replicate her family feasts). While Granny shared the love of the Lord with everyone in her family and her neighborhood, I've been blessed with opportunities to share it with others around the world in my speaking and ministry activities. I know that would please her.

Yes, there are differences in the way I do things and how Granny did them. Mama T's kitchen operation is quite a bit different than Mama Harrell's was. So I'll also share some of the lessons I've learned on my own, sprinkling in some of my streamlined cooking tips and a recipe or two along the way. I'll also stir in a good portion of spiritual food gleaned from God's Word.

By the time we're finished, I hope you'll feel as though you've dropped by, like my friend Shirley did, and sat down at my kitchen table to visit and to have an entertaining and stimulating discussion. Like Shirley, you won't leave with a full stomach—sorry I couldn't package up this book with a big mess of Mama T's famous turnip greens for you—but I hope your heart will be running over with a fresh understanding of God's love and your mind will be churning with new ideas for creating fun memories and leaving a lasting legacy to your family and friends.

And one last thing. Just to set the record straight, I have a couple of college degrees, and so does my editor. We've learned our grammar lessons; we know there "ain't no such word as ain't"—and a whole lot of other rules too. But listen up, honey: around my kitchen table, we serve it up family style. That means we say it however it sounds best, and if it sounds best with bad grammar and made-up words then, sister, that's how you're gonna get it. If you need something interpreted, contact me through my Web site, www.thelmawells.com, or call my office at 800-843-5622, and we'll try to explain it to you—and share a laugh while we're doing it.

2

Listen for God's Still, Small Voice

Wise people can also listen and learn;
even smart people can find good advice in these words.

—Proverbs 1:5 ncv

When our daughter Vikki called me during a Women of Faith conference somewhere, a flash of worry streaked through my mind as her number appeared on my cell phone's caller ID screen. Vikki was nearing the end of what had been a very difficult first pregnancy, and I knew she wouldn't call me during a conference unless it was something important.

"Hi, baby," I said, answering the call backstage. "How ya doin'?"

"Mama, I can see my ankles!" Vikki happily told me.

"You can see your ankles? Oh, thank you, Jesus! Thank you, Lord!" I cried, blinking back tears and lifting my face toward heaven.

Why all the excitement about Vikki's ankles? Well, if you saw Vikki while she and her sister Lesa performed as worship dancers at Women of Faith conferences, you know she is a beautiful, slim, agile young woman who looks like she'd have a hard time getting a scale to read a hundred pounds. But toward the end of her pregnancy, her legs and feet had become grossly swollen; they looked like big, tightly inflated L-shaped balloons. Her blood pressure shot up, and on the day before I'd left for that conference, her doctor told her he was going to put her in the hospital if things didn't improve.

So she had gone to bed, as he instructed (and she'd also taken a bit of her mama's home-remedy advice—swallowing a teaspoon of vinegar every morning). That day she was calling to tell me the good news. The swelling had gone down, and her ankles had reappeared. It was a great relief for all of us and sure made it easier for me to get through that weekend far from home.

But less than a week later, other problems popped up, and Vikki did wind up in the hospital. The next three days were filled with anticipation, questions, prayer, praise, worship, Bible reading, listening to doctors, getting additional opinions, and watching medical monitors. And through it all I anxiously watched as Vikki and her husband, James, went through the hardest phase of their life.

Never have I been so thankful for a physician who is a devout Christian as I was when the hospital's chief of obstetrics finally said to my daughter, "Vikki, listen to the still, small voice of God. He's telling you it's time to have this baby."

Vikki, James, and I were convinced that God was speaking through this doctor, and we all agreed it was time for the baby to be born—ready or not! As a result, beautiful little Marsaille Victoria Tennard entered this world that night weighing 5 pounds 12 ounces.

Praise God! Mother, Daddy, baby—and Grammy—have finally recovered from that nerve-racking ordeal, and we're all doing well now. But we won't forget the amazing things that happened during that experience; they illustrate the first lesson I want to share with you in this book: *listen for the Lord's voice.*

During her most stressful hospital hours, Vikki sang songs of praise, recited Scripture verses, called on Jesus and asked for His mercy, then listened for that still, small voice of God and followed his lead. And so did I. At one point during Vikki's ordeal, I started getting anxious and had to stop myself and pray, "Lord, you've told me to be anxious for nothing. In fact, I've gone all over the country telling people you've told us to be anxious for *no-thing*. Is this one of those *no-things* I shouldn't be anxious for?"

To be honest, given the difficulties Vikki was experiencing, I wouldn't have been too surprised if the answer had been, *No, Thelma, you've got good reason to worry. I want you to prepare yourself for a challenging situation. This isn't a no-thing. This is SOME-thing. This is your child and your grandchild.*

But that's not what happened, of course. When I asked God, "Is this a be-anxious-for-no-thing?" I sensed his voice resounding in my spirit: *Yes!*

Then the message of Psalm 138:8 came to my mind: *The Lord will fulfill his purpose for Vikki; your love, O Lord, endures forever.*

Glory be to God for his holy Word. I became totally peaceful and did not question God anymore.

Listening for That Still, Small Voice

Just as the doctor told Vikki during this crisis to listen to the still, small voice of God, we *all* need to listen for his voice every day in everything we do. We think of God as a majestic, omniscient being seated upon his glorious throne in heaven—and he is. But with that image fixed in our minds, we expect his words to come thundering down to us as roaring pronouncements accompanied by bolts of lightning. And sometimes maybe we *do* discern his will in the life storms that jerk us up out of our ordinary days and make us stop and ask, "Lord, are you trying to get my attention?"

But most of the time, I think God speaks to us softly, as he spoke to Elijah during one of the prophet's most trying times. He was running for his life and had hidden in a cave on Mount Horeb when God told him to go outside and wait on the mountainside, and he would pass by. What happened next probably wasn't what Elijah expected:

A hurricane wind ripped through the mountains and shattered the rocks before GOD, but GOD wasn't to be found in the wind; after the wind an earthquake, but GOD wasn't in the earthquake; and after the earthquake fire, but GOD wasn't in the fire; and after the fire a gentle and quiet whisper.

When Elijah heard the quiet voice, he muffled his face with his great cloak, went to the mouth of the cave, and stood there. A quiet voice asked, "So Elijah, now tell me, what are you doing here?" (1 Kings 19:11–13 MSG)

I've written this book to share with you, friend to friend, a few powerful and practical lessons I've learned throughout my life. I've given it a bossy title—*Listen Up, Honey*—because I really want you to pay attention so you can effortlessly gain the knowledge that I may have had to go through terrible trials and tears to get. But before you even think of listening to Thelma Wells, I want you to settle down with the Word of God and absorb *his* lessons. I want you to open your heart in prayer and listen for *his* voice whispering into your spirit.

Now, if you have one of those Type A, ants-in-your-pants personalities and you have a problem when it comes to paying attention, it may take you a while to learn how to clear your mind and focus on meditating and listening. But keep working at it, and eventually you'll notice you're able to spend an increasing amount of time with your heart tuned in to God. And once you've learned to sense his presence, you'll start looking and listening for God's will throughout your day.

For example, someone said that we all see situations

where we could do something good, but often as soon as we think of helping, another thought pushes its way into our heads, telling us our help isn't necessary. Or isn't wise. Or might be insulting. When that argument comes into your thinking, this person said, you can believe that the first thought to do good came from God, and the thought arguing against doing it came from, well, it didn't come from God.

While watching the anguish of those who lost everything in last year's terrible hurricanes, maybe you thought, *I really ought to send a donation to one of those relief organizations.* But while you were digging through your purse trying to find your checkbook, maybe another thought popped up: *You know, some of those organizations just can't be trusted; maybe I ought to rethink this.* Or, *There are people right here in my neighborhood who need help too.*

Now, those opposing thoughts can have merit; it's always wise to think things through before we put on our Florence Nightingale costumes and go tearing out to save the world. And certainly there *are* people in need everywhere we look. So if you chose to use your time and your resources closer to home, that's fine. But too often the opposing thought comes to us, and we end up not doing any good at all. When you learn to recognize and heed

God's "gentle and quiet whisper," you'll have more confidence that what you're doing *is* his will, and you'll find ways to serve others in his name with great energy and enthusiasm.

The apostle Paul knew all about the power that comes from listening to God. He told the Christians in Ephesus he was asking God "to make you intelligent and discerning in knowing him personally, your eyes focused and clear, so that you can see exactly what it is he is calling you to do, grasp the immensity of this glorious way of life he has for Christians, oh, the utter extravagance of his work in us who trust him—endless energy, boundless strength!" (Ephesians 1:17–19 MSG).

Today that same intelligence and discernment, that same endless energy and boundless strength, are still available to us when we listen for God's direction. I'm living proof of it!

*A*s I worked in the kitchen with Granny, we talked and laughed. She told me Bible stories, and I told her *everything.* As I got older and moved into adolescence and the teenage years, she wouldn't agree with some of the things I told her, but I knew I could always tell her whatever was on my mind, and she would listen.

If I told her something she didn't like, she might get very quiet. Looking back, I'm sure that in her quietness she was praying for wisdom on how to deal with me. She was more than sixty years old while she was rearing me, and I'm sure it was quite a culture shock to have a child in the household again after all the years since she had reared her two sons.

Sometimes when I would pour out a problem to Granny, she would say, "Sleep on the problem, child, and it'll be better in the morning." This lesson may seem trite, but Granny said it, and I've proved it to be true many times. One of the most beautiful of the Bible's Proverbs is 4:6: "Do not forsake wisdom, and she will protect you; love her, and she will watch over you" (NIV). Isn't that a beautiful image? I love to think of God's gift of wisdom watching over me, clearing my mind, as I "sleep on a problem."

Granny taught me not to make snap decisions when emotions are high and pressures are great. "Sleep on it, baby," she would tell me.

My experience in following Granny's advice leads me to believe that while we are sleeping God has an opportunity to speak to us subconsciously and delete the junk from our minds that needs to be trashed. Perhaps that's why so many people say they can think more clearly in the morning after a good night's rest.

Listening Brings Wisdom

In 2002 I was living an active, rewarding life, and while I'd set some goals for myself that were still a long way from being fulfilled, for the most part, I was content. I had really never had the urge to go back to school and get a graduate degree. In fact, I had always said I would *never* go back to school again. I didn't need to go back; I didn't want to go back; I didn't have time to go back.

I started a mentoring group called Daughters of Zion, and a lot of the people in that group had advanced degrees—one even had a PhD—but that didn't bother me a bit. I was happy for those people, and besides, in that group, we had all agreed that titles and credentials were left at the door, and everyone who came was on the same level. Going back to school was the furthest thing from my mind.

But one day I was sitting at my computer, and an advertisement appeared for Master's Divinity School. Usually I just delete that stuff. But that day I sat there thinking, *Hmmmm, Master's Divinity School. I wonder what this is.* So I clicked on it, it opened up, and there was all the information describing what this graduate school offered, blah-blah-blah-blah.

But a funny thing happened. The longer I looked, the more I liked what I saw. At the same time I was thinking, *I'm not going back to school. But it can't hurt to just see what's involved. Maybe I'll just fill out this little thing, this application.*

In my spirit, a quiet voice whispered, *Do it.*

So I filled out the application, sent it in—and the next thing I knew, I got a reply saying I'd been accepted.

I sat there looking at my computer screen and said, "What? I don't *want* to be accepted! I don't want to go back to school."

I called Vikki and said, "Vikki, I filled out this application for this graduate school, and now they've sent me back a message saying I've been accepted. But I don't want to go to graduate school."

She said, "Mama, do it."

Here's a second voice saying, Do it.

So I wrote in again and got the financial information. Next I sent them all the books I've written to see if the school would grant me some academic credit for the work I'd already done. They wrote back and said they only gave undergraduate credit for qualifying books, not graduate credit. I thought, *Shucks*.

I started the coursework. It came to me by mail, and the more I got into it, the more I enjoyed it. In fact, I loved the material I was given to study.

One day the president of Master's Divinity School called me. He said, "Mrs. Wells, I see that you're a student in our graduate school, and my wife and I went on a cruise with you this month."

I said, "Excuse me, sir. But you must have me mixed up with someone else. I haven't been on a cruise this month."

He laughed and told me that they had taken along all the books and materials I had sent to the school hoping to get graduate credit for them. He said, "We watched your videos, and we read your books, and now I have a question for you: Have you ever thought about writing curricula for schools?"

I said, "Sir, I *have* written a curriculum, but it was a

long time ago, and it was developed for an after-school program. I appreciate the inquiry, but I don't want to write curriculum. I don't have time to write curriculum. All I want to do is get my master's degree."

He said, "Oh, Sister Wells, you need to pray about that."

I said, "OK, I'll pray—but NO."

He said, "Well, let's just see what the Lord is going to do."

Later that month I got another call from the school's president. He said, "Let me be the first to congratulate you."

I said, "Oh?"

He said, "Yes, you don't need to write a curriculum. You've already written it. We want to take your book *Girl, Have I Got Good News for You* and use it to develop a course that we'll call Biblical Template for Counseling Hurting Women." Then he added, "Sister Wells, we've never had a female professor. We want to start a women's issues division with your material and have you lead the class."

I told him, "I can't be a professor. I don't have a master's degree—I'm still working on it."

He said, "You're working on your master's degree,

but you already know the Master. And if you'll agree, we'd like to go ahead with this plan."

Isn't that something?

Well, I eventually got my graduate degree, and guess who was invited to give the commencement address: me!

Now I'm enjoying my role in helping others achieve the same goal I started on when I listened to that gentle and quiet voice whispering *Do it* into my spirit. When students enroll in my course, the school sends them a four-part module based on *Girl, Have I Got Good News for You*: a workbook, an audiotape, a videotape, and the facilitator's guide. They select a person to do the study with them, then they work through the material together. It's self-paced, and when they finish the work, they send it to me, and I grade it.

Once a year I teach an accelerated course in person; it's usually at an off-campus site the school hosts in an appealing area in Florida. People come to enjoy the warm weather and to enroll in these courses. This kind of teaching has been a wonderful experience for me—and I hope it's rewarding for them as well.

Now, I started off saying degrees and titles didn't matter in my mentoring program, and they still don't. But at the same time, I think all of us in the program are inspired to see someone accomplish a goal he or she has set, no matter what that goal is. We celebrate and congratulate each other on our achievements.

Seek Wisdom

We can learn a lot simply by listening to God—and also by listening to others who are willing to teach us. You probably know the story of King Solomon. He was trying to rule over a population that was so big it seemed to Solomon "as numerous as the dust of the earth" (2 Chronicles 1:9 NIV). He needed great resources to deal with this vast kingdom, but when he prayed to God, he didn't ask for gold or silver. He asked for "wisdom and knowledge."

God was tremendously pleased with Solomon's request. He told the king:

> Because this was in your heart, and you have not asked riches or wealth or honor or the life of your enemies, nor have you asked long life—but have asked wisdom and knowledge for yourself, that you may judge My people over whom I have made you king— wisdom and knowledge are granted to you; and I will give you riches and wealth and honor, such as none of

the kings have had who were before you, nor shall any after you have the like. (vv. 11–12)

Solomon could have had anything he wanted—*anything*—yet he asked for wisdom so he would know how to be the best king he could be to God's people. In response, God made him the wisest man in all the world—*and* the richest!

King Solomon lived thousands of years ago, but the lesson learned from his story is just as valid today as it was back then. When we seek God's wisdom so that we can selflessly serve him and represent him in our world, he rewards us in ways we could never even think to ask for.

When I read the story of Solomon, I'm inspired to listen and to learn. I'm also intrigued by another character who entered the picture. In studying these Scripture passages, I've decided that if Solomon was the wisest man, the queen of Sheba had to be the wisest woman. Why? Because when she heard about King Solomon's wisdom, she loaded up a huge caravan and made her way to Jerusalem to listen and learn from him.

She was amazed by what he told her. She said, "I did not believe what they said until I came and saw with my own eyes. Indeed, not even half the greatness of your wisdom was told me; you have far exceeded the report I heard" (2 Chronicles 9:6 NIV).

Let's be like the queen of Sheba and seek out wisdom, even if it seems inconvenient or even if we think we're too busy or too old or already smart enough. Let's keep our spirits tuned to the frequency of the still, small voice of God giving us guidance and knowledge. Let's listen and learn.

Seek Wisdom!

Someone told me an interesting story about a minister who wanted to impart some wisdom to his congregation. To illustrate his point, he dropped four worms into four separate jars. The first worm was put into a jar of alcohol. The second worm was put into a jar of cigarette smoke. The third worm was put into a jar of chocolate syrup. The fourth worm was put into a jar of good, clean soil.

At the conclusion of his sermon, the minister showed his congregation the results: the worm in alcohol was dead, the worm in cigarette smoke was dead, and the worm in chocolate syrup was dead. But the worm he had placed in good, clean soil was still alive.

"So," the minister asked, "what can we learn from this lesson?"

A little old woman in the back raised her hand and said, "As long as you drink, smoke, and eat chocolate, you won't have worms!"

Mama T says, Listen up, honey. As long as you listen to the gentle and quiet voice of God whispering into your heart, you can bottle up those worms of worry and know that the King of kings will guide you with wisdom and love through whatever lies ahead. Connect with him. Feel his presence in your life. When you do, "Your ears shall hear a word behind you, saying, 'This is the way, walk in it'" (Isaiah 30:21).

3

Leave a Legacy:
Sundays at Mama T's

Just make sure you stay alert. Keep close watch over yourselves. Don't forget anything of what you've seen. Don't let your heart wander off. Stay vigilant as long as you live. Teach what you've seen and heard to your children and grandchildren.

—Deuteronomy 4:9 msg

Sometimes Sundays at Grammy and Papa's house start on Wednesday. If our family is going to gather at our house on Sunday and I'm leaving on Thursday for a Women of Faith conference somewhere, then Wednesday's the day I get everything ready. I buy all the groceries we'll need and get the meat ready. Generally I choose a big brisket, and I rub it all over with seasoning then put it in a big, covered roasting pan and stick it in the refrigerator out in the garage. Sometimes I make my famous five-cup salad (I'll share the recipe later in this chapter), and I set out all the stuff we'll need for the usual Wells family feast.

I have a good time at the conference, buzzing through my presentations and enjoying the chance to meet and chat with all the women who stop by my book table to say hello. Then, early Sunday morning, I take the first flight out, hoping to make it home in time for eleven o'clock church. Sometimes I call George, my husband, from the airport and remind him to put the meat in the oven.

Then, after church, the family descends on us—our three grown kids and their families and sometimes some friends and other relatives too. The front door swings open, and here come anywhere from ten to twenty-five of them, led by the grandkids—and the first place the youngsters go is to my bedroom, where they pull off their Sunday clothes and rummage through my closet. Uh-huh. They're spoiled. I let 'em do just about anything at my house, and one of their favorite "anythings" is playing dress-up in Grammy's closet. Now, they don't go *totally* wild in there. I've told them what they can and cannot play with, and I've taught them to pick up and hang up my things after they're done playing (well, OK, we're still working on that lesson). They have a grand time playing their own giggle-filled version of *What Not to Wear* and other silly, made-up scenarios, and they love to act out runway fashion shows for us.

The men head for the den or the exercise room, depending on whether they want to watch sports (that would be in the exercise room—where more eating gets done than exercising), and others head for the den if they're going to watch a movie or something else on TV.

George heads for his favorite chair, the comfortable, green La-Z-Boy recliner. Everyone knows that's his chair, and heaven help anyone else who tries to sit in it—except for the little granddaughters. Every once in a while a couple of them will decide to challenge him. Two or three of them will plop down there with sweet, innocent looks on their faces like they have no idea they've entered forbidden territory. Then one of them will say, "Shhhh! Here comes Papa!"

George will stride into the room, stand over his beloved chair with his hands on his hips, and say, "You little gals get outta my chair."

The girls squirm and giggle, and then the most amazing thing happens: George moves on to another chair! Oh, those granddaughters. It's just too hard to resist their giggly charm. Other times they'll get up and George will sit down—then they'll pile on top of him!

So the men and children are scattered all over the house, and you *know* where the women are. We go straight to the kitchen. One turns on the burners to heat up the food that's waiting on the stove. One turns on or off the oven, depending on what the meat's status is. Another puts ice in the punch bowl. Usually she dumps about half of it on the table and the floor and has to go get the broom and dustpan to clean up the mess. (I'll tell you a little secret about that punch bowl a little later.) We're all busy, talk-ing, passing, stirring, slicing—getting everything ready.

Pretty soon one of the granddaughters strolls in, all decked out in Grammy's finery, and whines, "I'm HON-gry! When we gonna eat?" Bless her heart. She can't wait to fill her mouth with all that good food.

So finally we're ready, and we all gather in the kitchen. The little kids will eat first, so they say their prayer together: "God is great; God is good. Let us thank him for our food. By his hands we are fed; give us, Lord, our daily bread."

And just as they start to say "Amen," there's one who adds, big and loud, "The LORRRRRRD is my shepherd! I SHALL not want . . ."

One of the adults will interrupt and say, "Honey, this is grace, not recitation time," but that hardly stops her. On she goes with steady, steely resolve: "He MAKETH ME to lie down in GREEEEEEEEN pastures . . ."

That girl *will* complete her psalm, so the rest of us give up and wait. Now, I have to admit, that little granddaughter takes after her Grammy. On special occasions, like birthdays or holidays or other special times, I'll follow the kids' prayer with one of my own. And, believe it or not, I sometimes tend to go on a little long too. In fact, Lesa's husband, Patrick, always jokes (honey, he'd *better* be joking!), "Don't ask Mama T to pray. The food is gonna get cold!" But like my little granddaughter, I just keep on praying and praising and thanking the Lord for this wild bunch that has descended upon me.

We fill the kids' plates and settle them down in whatever room they've chosen to eat in that day. Sometimes we women fill the men's plates for them. One of the things Granny taught me was never to start something I didn't want to continue doing again and again. I learned what she meant shortly after George and I were married. At some church dinner or family event, I filled George's plate for him. And at the next church dinner or family picnic, he expected me to fix his plate for him again! I could see this was going to be a habit. But you know what? I decided that was something I didn't mind doing, and now, all these years later, I fill George's plate for him when we're at family gatherings. I know what he likes (and, just between you and me, what he should and shouldn't eat), and I fix his plate and take it to him.

The men settle into the den or the exercise room. And we women, well, we gather around the kitchen table, of course. It's supposed to seat four, but by the time we're ready to eat, there may be eight or more of us squeezed in there.

If we have extra people, the overflow gathers around the table of last resort—the one in the dining room!

I'm not sure what goes on in the other rooms, but in the kitchen, we women solve *all* the world's problems as we eat and share and laugh and tease. With my daughters and daughter-in-law and maybe some other friends and family gathered around me, we discuss the best way to do everything from taking care of the nation to mopping the floor. We have a lot of cares and concerns, and we try to work those out. You see, the women in our family have a lot of wonderful minds, and we know what *you* should do and how you should do it. Sometimes, when one of us is going through a difficult time, we join hands and pray for each other. We share favorite passages we've read from the Bible, and we talk about our favorite shows on TV.

The truth is, of course, at the end of our sometimes loud and colorful dinner conversation, when we finally get up from the table with a groan and set about cleaning up the kitchen, we may not have solved any real problems at all, but we've accomplished something wonderful all the same. We've leaned on each other, we've held each other up, and we've loved each other. At the end of that meal, our hearts are as full with love for each other as our stomachs are full of the good food we've just eaten.

On those special Sundays, when our house is filled with the happy, contented sounds of people who love each other and love to eat, I usually find myself sitting back and soaking up the sounds as I silently thank God for giving me this extraordinary blessing. The words of Proverbs 17:6 often come to mind: "Grandchildren are the crowning glory of the aged; parents are the pride of their children" (NLT).

Now, I don't consider myself "aged," at least not yet. But I know for sure that my grandchildren are my "crowning glory," and I strive to live my life in a Christlike way that will always bring pride, and never shame, to my family. That's not to say our bunch is perfect. Honey, I could tell you about challenges and heartache and despair we've been through that would make you wonder how we ever survived with our sanity intact—or maybe it would explain why our sanity sometimes seems to have left the building! I know all about hard times, sister. But those times just make these good times all the sweeter.

More than Meat and Potatoes

Why am I telling you about the wild Wells-family food fest? Because one of the lessons I want to share with my family—and with you—is the importance of creating memories and leaving a legacy. Years from now—or who knows? maybe tomorrow—when I'm up in heaven sitting at the Lord's lavish banquet table, I want my children and grandchildren and great-grandchildren to think of me whenever the family gathers. I hope they'll remember Grammy or Mama T as one who showed them how to have a constantly abiding love for the Lord, a headstrong devotion to family, a passion for overcoming challenges, a zest for living, and a craving for laughter. In the way I live my life—but especially in those Sunday gatherings—that's the legacy I'm working to establish.

So in the rest of this chapter, I want to share some specifics about a few of the steps that go into these family gatherings. Nothing profound, just some little hints and tips. Maybe they'll give you ideas for how you can establish or embellish your own legacy of sharing the Lord, love, and laughter with your family—or with your neighborhood.

I know a lot of you have families that are scattered all over the country. The ideas here can help you make the most of your family times when you do get together without wearing yourself ragged. And if your neighbors or church friends are your "family," I hope you'll find these ideas helpful in hosting occasional gatherings that bring you and your friends together for fellowship and mutual nurturing.

The Easy Way: Mama T's Lightbulb Moment

I've already told you about the way my Granny did things. She didn't cut corners, and neither do I. Honey, I cut so there's hardly anything left *but* the corner! You see, I travel nearly thirty weekends a year with Women of Faith, and I run two ministries and write books and do all sorts of other things. So if there's a quick-and-easy way to do something, that's the Mama T way.

For starters, let me tell you the key word in hosting an informal get-together: *plastic*. Back in the old days, before

I got smart, I refused to allow anything plastic in my house. That's right. Paper plates were for picnics, and I don't like flies and ants, so I don't do picnics! I used my fine china and crystal every time I had company. And let me tell you, I have some nice stuff. I loved sitting at the dining room table with my guests (before it became the eating place of last resort) and looking out over all the brightly polished gold flatware, the twinkling crystal glasses, the gleaming china plates and serving pieces, the sparkling chafing dishes, and the perfectly pressed cloth napkins. But as time went on, making sure all that stuff was polished and twinkling and gleaming and sparkling and pressed got to be a real drag, and I ain't kiddin'! I was working myself silly, and I even started dreading these get-togethers instead of delighting in them. In short, as my family grew with the addition of in-laws and grandkids—I grew tired!

Plus, I didn't want my grandkids to come to my house and hear me telling them all the time, "Don't touch that!" "Don't drop that!" "Be careful!" When our children were small, we had a relative like that, and whenever we went to her house, she spent the whole time fussing at the kids, worried they would break her stuff. And you know what? The only place we went where my kids ever broke things was her house. We were all so nervous and on edge around her, it just seemed inevitable.

So one Sunday, after everyone had left and I was still in the kitchen washing and drying and putting away all the china and crystal and silver, I gave myself a good talkin' to. I said, "Thelma, you got up at 5 a.m. in Pittsburgh, flew several hundred miles, went to church, put on a feast for your family, and now it's nearly 9 p.m. and you're still in the kitchen. What are you thinkin', girl? You're runnin' yourself into the ground—and you're way too smart for that. Get yourself some plastic plates and flatware and cups and napkins and a big ol' trash can, and next time you put on a feed for your family, you use that stuff and you just *see* if the world comes to an end."

Well, guess what. That's what I did. And although it bothered me a little at first, it didn't seem to bother anyone else—especially the women who helped with the cleanup. So now for our Sunday gatherings, I use plastic and paper everything: cups, plates, flatware, napkins. Even the punch bowl is plastic. (But that's my secret; everyone who looks at it thinks it's crystal.) I use it because it's the perfect size for mixing my secret-recipe fruit tea (sorry, honey, that's one recipe I just don't share), and we ladle it right out of that fancy-looking plastic punch bowl with a fancy-looking plastic ladle into ordinary plastic cups. And so far, no one has suffered death by plasticide. So, girl-friend, if you want to get me a present, don't send me a crystal bowl or fancy serving plate or a set of linen nap-kins. You just send me some plastic!

And here's something else: we serve the food directly from the stove. Uh-huh. I know. Martha Stewart would probably sic the hospitality police on me if she knew I was committing this major faux pas, but, sister, when you serve from the stove, the food stays warm for all the refills, and Mama T and the girls don't have all those big serving bowls to wash when dinner is over. We women stand around the kitchen, and we fill the kids' plates. Then we fill the men's plates. Then we fill our own plates. And that's just the way we do it.

Now, I'm not saying I've permanently retired my good china, crystal, and flatware. At Christmastime and on other special occasions, I'll put on a fine spread with all the shining-twinkling-gleaming-and-pressed stuff, and that dining table (yes, sometimes we still do use it) looks like something out of a magazine. You see, I do want my grandkids to appreciate nice things. That's what Granny taught me, and I'm passing on the lesson to my family. Even though we were poor and lived in that little shack of an apartment, Granny had some beautiful china and crystal, and she taught me to cherish and appreciate the few good things she had.

So on holidays or birthdays, I'll do it up right, and we'll all sit around the table in our Sunday clothes and have a high-class, multicourse meal. And if someone breaks something, well, it can be replaced. If it can't be replaced and it's important to me, then I don't put it out for the grandkids to use. (But I've learned that adults tend to break just as many things as kids do. I've also learned to get over it; after all, it's just stuff.)

The Menu: Girl, We're Talkin' Soul Food

OK, now for the menu. A typical Sunday dinner at Mama T's house might include some or all of the following:

Brisket. In places outside Texas, roast beef is probably more common, but either way, it's a big hunk of beef cooked with potatoes, onions, and carrots. As I mentioned earlier, I often get the meat ready on Wednesday if I have to be away for a Women of Faith conference. I get a brisket big enough to feed at least ten people or more, depending on how many I'm expecting. I wash it (Granny taught me to wash *everything* before cooking it; I've even been known to wash hamburger), trim off the excess fat, and rub it—more like massaging it—with seasoning salt (I like Mrs. Dash brand), then garlic powder, then onion powder, then pepper. I put it on a rack in the roasting pan, and sometimes I scatter some cut cloves of garlic over it too. Then of course I put it back in the refrigerator. On Sunday morning, George will add a couple of cups of water to the pan and some cut-up onions before he sticks it into a 350-degree oven. Generally the size of brisket we get needs four hours or so to cook. Before he leaves for church, he'll turn down the oven to 250 degrees. When we get home from church, I'll toss in some carrots and some cut-up, peeled potatoes, and I may turn the oven back up so they'll cook while we're getting everything else ready.

Tossed salad. I buy the salad in a bag and add raisins, bacon bits, and sometimes cheese; then I'll put some chopped pecans or slivered almonds on the side (because some of the grandkids won't eat nuts). My favorite salad dressing is to mix Kraft vinaigrette and Kraft ranch in roughly equal parts. Delicious!

Five-cup salad. I usually make this on Wednesday, too, because it gets better the longer it sits. You'll need one large cup of canned mandarin oranges, one cup of pineapple chunks or tidbits, a small tub of sour cream, a bag of miniature marshmallows, and the same size bag of shredded coconut. Drain the juice from the canned oranges and pineapple, and put them in a bowl. Mix in the marshmallows and coconut. Add the sour cream last. I wash my hands really good and use them to do the mixing so I can feel the consistency and know I'm coating and mixing everything really well. Then stick it in the refrigerator, and let your mouth water for four days as you think about eating it on Sunday. Sometimes I make a double batch; it'll keep a couple of weeks in the refrigerator. People who don't have picky grandkids add nuts to it too—pecans or walnuts.

Cooked greens. I buy the fresh ones in the bag, already cut up and washed (and I'm just glad Granny isn't alive to see me do it). Of course, I wash mine again. You can choose mustard greens, turnip greens, or collards, and they're all delicious. I put them in a big pot with water, salt, pepper, chopped onion, and a ham hock if I've got one. Then I stir in that magical ingredient: bacon grease. Just a spoonful. Now don't you go shaking your head at me, girl. If you're gonna eat greens, you've gotta add bacon grease. A little bit won't hurt you. I always say the vitamins in the greens cancel out the cholesterol. Absolutely.

Green beans. Whether I start with canned or frozen, I wash them first (of course). Then I put water on the stove to boil, and in that water I put some chopped onion and sprinkle in some seasonings—pepper and some Season-All Seasoned Salt—and a quarter stick of real butter. (Now, don't start whinin' about that butter. I told you this is *soul* food, honey. You can diet Monday through Saturday, but remember that Sunday is the day of rest—and at my house that means on Sunday we eat all the *rest* of the stuff we can't eat on those other dieting days!) Finally, I stir in the green beans and let them boil until they're hot and tender.

Granny's Green Beans

There was a vacant lot near our apartment back in the alley, and Granny had a little garden there. Every summer morning, while it was still cool, she got up early and worked in her garden. Now, when I look back in my memory and see her standing there among the rows of green beans and okra, a phrase from the book of Genesis comes to mind. It says how

Adam and Eve "heard the sound of the LORD God walking in the garden in the cool of the day" (3:8). Isn't that a pleasant image? God and Granny both liked to walk—and work—in their gardens. God called his good, and so did Granny.

One of my favorite foods at Granny's house was her green beans with new potatoes. Oh my goodness, they were good! She'd pick the fresh green beans—it would never have occurred to her to use canned or frozen—and she would wash them ever so carefully. Then she'd wash the new potatoes. Girl, by the time she got done with them, she'd about scrubbed all the red off. She scrubbed them with a Brillo pad!

Next she put some water in a pot and put it on the stove to boil; she seasoned the boiling water with salt, pepper, and a ham hock if she had one. If she didn't, she'd add a little bacon grease. Next she would cut up an onion and add that. Then she added the green beans, and after they'd cooked awhile, she added the new potatoes, and they would cook alllllll morning. Honey, I didn't know you could steam green beans and eat them crunchy until I was probably thirty years old! Granny's green beans were *cooked.* And just before they were done, she'd add a pinch of sugar. She said sugar brings out the flavor of vegetables. She didn't add enough to make the beans sweet; she just wanted the flavor to burst. And, girlfriend, Granny made some *mean* green beans and new potatoes.

Corn. Here's a surprise: to cook an entire bag of frozen, whole-grain corn, I'll add just *one teaspoon* of water—the reason being that corn makes water. After it warms up and the water flows out of it, add a little salt and pepper, a pinch of sugar, and a quarter stick of butter.

Smothered cabbage. My family *loves* my smothered cabbage. Start by sautéing one chopped onion and one chopped bell pepper in butter. While it's sautéing, stir it constantly, and with your other hand, cut up the cabbage (just kidding; maybe you want to chop the cabbage first). Of course you've washed that onion and bell pepper and cabbage, haven't you? Yes, ma'am. Now cut the cabbage into sections, then start at the tip of the section and chop it up. You have to have a sharp knife and a good cutting board for this. Don't chop it in a food processor; that shreds it too fine. You want a texture that's more like cubes than slaw. Now pour a little water or a small can of beef or chicken broth in the pan where the veggies are sautéing, sprinkle in a scant teaspoon of sugar, add the cabbage, put a lid on the pan, turn the heat down low, and let it smother. It needs to cook about ten minutes or so, not much more, because you want it to be a little crunchy.

Cornbread. I can give you this recipe in fewer than ten words: Jiffy cornbread mix baked in a cast-iron skillet.

Parker House rolls. I have a good excuse for not making these rolls from scratch: Granny never taught me how. But the frozen ones, the kind packaged in a tin cake pan, are almost as good.

Mama T's secret tea. Nope, I'm still not tellin'.

Desserts. Often the girls will bring some sweets, and sometimes we rev up the electric freezer and make homemade ice cream. On special occasions, I might make a strawberry cake. (You'll find the recipe in chapter 7.)

Soaking Up the Joy

Are you hungry yet? I sure am! But more than feeling hungry for *food*, I'm hungry for *family*. I want to have my

husband and children and grandchildren and greatgrand-
child around me. I want to hug them and laugh with them
and pray with them. I want to feel my husband's kiss on
my face. I want to hear my daughters saying, "Love you,
Mama." I want to hear my grandchildren's laughter echo-
ing out of the closet as they pull on their dress-up costumes. I want to hear my sons-in-law say, "Oh, Mama T,
that sure was a good dinner."

That's the legacy my family leaves *me* after every family gathering, and it's also the legacy I want to leave them:
the memory of loved ones gathered together, laughing
and eating together, the feel of my arms wrapped around
each one of them, and the knowledge that our hearts are
joined in love for each other and love for the Lord.

Thank you, Jesus, for this family of mine!

I hope you'll thank Jesus for *your* family too—whoever and wherever they are. Even if the family you
claim as your own isn't "blood kin," if it's friends or
neighbors or church members or whoever, recognize
those dear ones as God's gift to you. Proverbs 18:24
says, "A true friend sticks by you like family" (MSG). So
if you've got friends, you've got family. And until we get
together in heaven with *all* our brothers and sisters in
Christ, our earthly families are the ones God has given

us to help us "keep on keepin' on" through all of life's joys and sorrows.

Get together with your friends and loved ones whenever you can. Spend time with them. Feel Christ's presence among you. He has told us he will be with us *always* (see Matthew 28:20), not just when we're sad and alone but also when we're happy and surrounded by loved ones.

You don't have to put on a feast. Order pizza. Get some Chinese takeout. Buy a couple of loaves of good, crusty bread and some deli meat and cheese, and let everyone make sandwiches. The food isn't the important thing. The warm memories you're creating, the love you're sharing, and the bonds you're building—those are priorities.

Admittedly, though, after I've spent the day with my family gathered around me, there always comes a time when I'm ready for my family to move on. On Sunday evening, I've been known to tell my bunch, "I am sick of y'all. Take your children and go home! Bye-bye. And don't leave nothin' either. You take your diaper bag and your cake plate and your purse and your sunglasses and your kids' clothes, and you get on home now."

Usually I say that around six o'clock . . . the first time. Then we find one more thing we need to talk about or do together, and the next thing I know it's eight o'clock and some stragglers are still there. I shoo them out again, and if I'm lucky, by eight-thirty the house is quiet, and I can finally head for my bubble bath, exhausted but still soaking up all the joy that's filled my house that day.

We all make choices every day. I could choose to sleep in on Sunday mornings in the Women of Faith conference city, catch a later flight home, skip church, and come home to a nice, quiet, peaceful place where I could spend the day resting and watching TV. But the way I see it, I'll have plenty of time to rest and relax when I go to my *eternal* rest. Every day I try to remember a beloved old passage from the book of Deuteronomy. I remember it, and I make a choice.

> I place before you Life and Death, Blessing and Curse. Choose life so that you and your children will live. And love GOD, your God, listening obediently to him, firmly embracing him. Oh yes, he is life itself, a long life settled on the soil that GOD, your God, promised to give your ancestors. (30:19–20 MSG)

I choose life—a full and rich and jam-packed life that leaves behind a legacy of love and inspiration for my family and friends. Which choice are *you* making?

4

Pass On to Others God's Indescribable Gift

My grace is sufficient for you, for My strength is made
perfect in weakness. . . . Therefore I take pleasure in infir-
mities, in reproaches, in needs, in persecutions, in distresses,
for Christ's sake. For when I am weak, then I am strong.

—2 CORINTHIANS 12:9–10

Now, let's push back from the dinner table and talk about some other lessons I've learned over the years. Like I said, I learned a lot of them the hard way. One of them happened after a woman—I'll call her Mrs. Carter—heard me speak at her company's national meeting. She liked what she heard, and she invited me to speak at her family's reunion. It was the first time the family had gathered in Dallas, and she wanted someone who was funny and charming, someone who would inspire and energize her family members. She enthusiastically told her relatives I was the perfect person for this auspicious occasion.

When Mrs. Carter introduced me that Saturday evening, she used words like *dynamic*, *wonderful*, and *hilarious*; she assured the audience members they would love and adore me. "Now sit back and relax," she gushed. "You're in for a real treat!"

With such an introduction, I stepped behind that podium fired up with energy, eager to fulfill Mrs. Carter's prediction. But something went wrong. Instead of being witty, funny, and charming, I was sour, condemning, and preachy! I heard myself scolding this gathering of fun-loving relatives about how men should take responsibility for their family and do what was right. I told them their wives depended on them to be the head of the house and that when the head of the house was sick the whole family suffered. I fumed about overcrowded prisons that are full of irresponsible men who had left their families to fend for themselves. In the back of my mind, I heard my brain telling my mouth to get a grip and change direction, but I wasn't listenin' to my brain. It might as well have been in someone else's head that night, for all the good it was doing *me!*

I was on a sour soapbox of anger, frustration, bitterness, and rage, and I dumped it all out on that innocent, unsuspecting family reunion. Why? Because I had just learned of an incident involving a young man whose irresponsibility had caused great damage to his family. This was a family I cared about, and the situation had caused me (and them) a lot of grief and pain. The turmoil of emotions resulting from that tragedy was foremost in my mind that evening as I looked out over my audience. As a result, I was determined to convince all the men in attendance to stop doing wrong (whether or not they *were* doing anything wrong), to establish the right environment in their home (whether or not they already had), and to stand tall and be the men God had made them to be.

My presentation was met with stony stares and raised eyebrows, especially from Mrs. Carter. There might have been a time and place to say such things, but that family reunion was neither. Despite those bad vibes, I just couldn't stop. I went on for forty-five minutes, and the longer I talked, the angrier I got, and the more accusatory I became. The audience was obviously uncomfortable, and Mrs. Carter was probably considering murder or suicide—or both! When I finally sat down, she took the microphone and said, "Well, that was *not* what I was promised—or expected!"

I was mortified. I sat there on the front row with my head bowed, unable even to look at her. As soon as I could, I fled to the restroom. Hiding behind the closed stall door, I could hear the other women in the restroom talking about how bad my speech had been. One lady said, "I hope she got her point across to the men. *Somebody* must have needed it." I slithered to my car and drove home in tears, wishing there was a cliff somewhere along the way I could drive off of!

God's Precious Gift: Gracious Forgiveness

The next day, I left a message on Mrs. Carter's answering machine, apologizing and asking her to call me back so I could tell her again how very sorry I was. I wanted so much to apologize, but Mrs. Carter never called me back. I wrote her a letter and tried in other ways to reach her, but I never made contact with her again. I can only image that even today, twenty years later, she shudders if she ever hears my name, remembering the torture I put her through! Similarly, I shudder remembering that awful presentation. I still wish I could apologize to her, but I know I got what I deserved from her: stony silence and the perpetual burden of knowing I caused her (and myself) severe embarrassment. It's as though, in Mrs. Carter's mind, I made a permanent mistake that can never be forgiven and so will never go away.

My shame took me to the Word of God, searching for solace. And of course I found it. In his second letter to the Corinthians, Paul described how a "thorn" in his flesh seemed like "a messenger of Satan" that tormented him. We don't know exactly what the "thorn" was, but it must have been a great burden, because Paul said he "pleaded with the Lord" to take it away.

In response, the Lord told him, "My grace is sufficient for you, for My strength is made perfect in weakness. . . . Therefore I take pleasure in infirmities, in reproaches, in needs, in persecutions, in distresses, for Christ's sake. For when I am weak, then I am strong" (2 Corinthians 12:9–10).

I've memorized that passage, and I call it to mind often whenever I need to relearn this lesson. My circumstances are different than Paul's, but there are similarities too. He was an itinerant apostle and later a martyr whose mission was to spread the gospel throughout the land. I'm just an itinerant speaker trying to bring glory to God in the way I earn my living. But I understand what it's like to have a "thorn" that causes pain, whether it's physical or emotional. And I'm, oh, so thankful that Jesus's grace is sufficient to ease my suffering from humiliation or anger or worry or any other problem I might have. Mrs. Carter might not accept my apology, but that's OK. Jesus will, and his gracious response is much more important to me than hers.

I deserved the icy response I got from Mrs. Carter for the mistake I made in delivering an inappropriate message to her family reunion. And I deserve a similar response every time I come running back to the Lord after I make yet another blunder. But the wonderful lesson is . . . with him, I *don't* get what I deserve! His grace is sufficient, and his patience is infinite. So no matter how many mistakes I make (and I don't know about you, sister, but I seem to be gifted in goofs!), I *know* his grace will be there, constant and free and waiting to give me another chance. What freedom we have, knowing that once God forgives us, our sin is gone from his memory.

Again and again the Bible tells us that we serve a gracious God who forgives us and loves us. One of the most beautiful of these passages is in Psalm 103:

The LORD is compassionate and gracious,
> slow to anger, abounding in love.
He will not always accuse,
> nor will he harbor his anger forever;
>> he does not treat us as our sins deserve
> or repay us according to our iniquities.
For as high as the heavens are above the earth,
> so great is his love for those who fear him;
> as far as the east is from the west,
> so far has he removed our transgressions from us.
As a father has compassion on his children,
> so the LORD has compassion on those who fear him;
> for he knows how we are formed,
> he remembers that we are dust. (vv. 8–14 NIV)

Isn't it comforting to know that, in God's eyes, our transgressions are no longer part of the landscape? Reading this passage, I picture a young child, running back to a loving father after the child has made some kind of foolish mistake, messing up in a way that would be stupid for an adult. "It's OK," this father says sympathetically, pulling the distraught child onto his lap and wiping away the tears. "You're just a kid, and kids make mistakes." In the same way, when I mess up, my Abba God pulls me into his everlasting arms and forgives me for my stupid errors. "It's OK," I imagine him telling me. "You're just dust, and dust makes mistakes."

The Hard Part: Passing On the Gift of Grace

Our fellow human beings may not be able to forgive us, and sometimes the mistakes we make on earth require that earthly justice must be served, but we can be assured that our Father's grace is sufficient to forgive our sins and give us a fresh start. That's the only way, in our weakened state of shame, we have the power to pick ourselves up and get going again.

I can't help but chuckle when I read on down in 2 Corinthians 12 and find, in verse 11, Paul fuming, "Well, now I've done it! I've made a complete fool of myself by going on like this" (MSG). He was referring to his own ranting and raving to the Corinthians about a completely different subject than my own sermonette in front of the family reunion, but it still makes me laugh whenever I read it, because he so perfectly described my own feelings after I had embarrassed myself.

Let's face it: we're going to mess up occasionally; it's just part of our weakness as human beings. But the Bible says when we need forgiveness we should "come boldly to the throne of grace, that we may obtain mercy and find grace to help in time of need" (Hebrews 4:16).

Imagine that! When we make a mistake, we aren't expected to grovel our way back into God's good graces. We're privileged to march up to his throne of grace *boldly*, not hanging back, not whimpering and whining, but *boldly* coming before him to "obtain mercy and find grace." Is our God a great God, or what?!

But here's the hard part, honey: God expects us to extend the same grace and forgiveness to those who offend us. That's right. We're supposed to forgive the ones who hurt us, insult us, wrong us, and come to our family reunions and present an angry tirade when we were expecting laughter and inspiration! Right there in the Lord's Prayer that we all surely pray on a regular basis, we say, "Forgive us our debts, as we forgive our debtors" (Matthew 6:12). In Luke's version of the prayer, it reads, "Forgive us our sins, for we also forgive everyone who is indebted to us" (11:4).

Mercy! Don't you wish he'd taught us something else? Don't you wish he'd said we're supposed to pray, "Forgive us our sins, Lord, and zap those who sin against us. Just let 'em have it. Blast 'em with your mighty power, Jesus.

Teach 'em a lesson. They oughta know better than to mess with us. After all, we're Christians!'"?

Let me just confess right here: sometimes I get mad at people, and I have a hard time getting over it. They did me *wrong*, girl! They hurt me, and I want to hurt them back. I want them to feel the same pain or humiliation or bigotry or dismay they put on me. But Jesus has told us to forgive those who sin against us: "Even if it's personal against you and repeated seven times through the day, and seven times he says, 'I'm sorry, I won't do it again,' forgive him" (Luke 17:4 MSG).

Still, like the apostle Paul, I sometimes "decide to do good, but I don't really do it. . . . My decisions, such as they are, don't result in actions. Something has gone wrong deep within me and gets the better of me every time" (Romans 7:19–20 MSG).

When those people who have wronged me come to mind, I *decide* to forgive them. I *will* myself to forgive them. But too often, the thing that "has gone wrong deep within me . . . gets the better of me."

I can't do it on my own, and I know I'm not the only one who feels this way. When Jesus told his disciples to forgive those who had wronged them, they replied, "Give us more faith" (Luke 17:5 MSG).

They asked for help, and so do I. "Help me do this thing that is so difficult to do," I beg.

Why did Jesus stress this lesson of forgiveness? Surely one reason is that we're Jesus's representatives on earth. When we hold ourselves up as Christians, others watch how we live our lives, and depending on what they see, they may or may not decide that they want to be Christians themselves.

My high school principal helped me learn this lesson years ago. He may not have thought of it as a biblical lesson, but it was. You see, in high school I was pretty smart, and I was fairly popular. I performed in almost all the school's musical assemblies, usually singing "Ave Maria." In my senior year, I ran for homecoming queen. But when they announced the winner, it wasn't me.

Very quickly, however, an insider told me I actually had won, but the title had been given to someone else. It was explained to me that the faculty member in charge of the election had a preference for marching-band twirlers; nobody could ever remember anybody but a twirler being elected homecoming queen. Well, I wasn't a twirler, and when I didn't win, I cried and I cried. I talked about the girl who did win—said some ugly things about her. I talked about her really bad because I was so hurt.

When he heard about my behavior, the principal, Dr. J. Leslie Patton, called me into his office. He was one of the most powerful, stately gentlemen I've ever known, and he had me sit down in front of his desk. Then he told me, "Miss Smith, I understand that you're upset because you didn't win homecoming queen—and rightfully so. You should be upset. But I'm going to tell you something. Ten years from today, nobody's going to care whether or not you were homecoming queen. What people will remember is how you conducted yourself when you lost. That is a part of your reputation that will follow you the rest of your life. So don't be angry and say things you'll be ashamed of later. You have a wonderful record; you're a model student. Being homecoming queen has nothing to do with your success. Forgive the ones you need to forgive. Put this incident behind you, and move on."

He gave me the sweetest talk—just beat me up all over with his good advice. And I've always remembered it. Now when my grandkids arrive at my house with a tearful expression on their faces, when they wearily plop down at my kitchen table (even they know it's the best place to have a talk) and pour out their hurts about something someone has done to them, some wrong they have endured, some contest they have lost, I pass along to them the advice Dr. Patton gave to me.

"Honey, I know it hurts right now. But it's not going to matter in the future whether you won this thing or not," I tell them. "It's not going to matter if so-and-so said something hurtful to you. What's going to matter is how you accepted the loss, how you responded to the one who hurt you. It's your choice to be angry or bitter and say hurtful things back to that person. It's also your choice to say, 'Oh well,' and move on. I know it's hard to forgive, but that's what the Lord tells us to do."

Doing the Impossible

My grandchildren (and several thousand other people) know that I have a great admiration for the bumblebee. I wear a bumblebee pin every single day of my life to remind myself and others that in Jesus Christ we can *bee* our best. It also reminds me to do what seems impossible, because, you see, there was a time when scientists were confounded by the fact that, aerodynamically, bumblebees shouldn't be able to fly. Their wings are too short, their bodies too big. But guess what: the bumblebee just goes right on buzzin' all over creation, because nobody ever told that fool it can't fly! It does what seems impossible. And that's what we do, too, when we accept the indescribable gift of grace and forgiveness from our Lord Jesus Christ—and then, with his help, pass it on to others.

I'm fascinated by bumblebees and also by their cousins, the honeybees. In the darkness of the hive—and in the bright sunlight of the day—honeybees go about their work with a steadfast devotion that's hard to comprehend.

But there's something else about the honeybee besides its work that can teach us an important lesson. Did you know that when a honeybee stings someone, the sting is *always* fatal to the bee?

In *The Bee Book*, writer Daphne More explains that the bee's stinger is barbed, and when the bee thrusts the stinger into "the comparatively thick human skin the bee cannot withdraw it. It twirls about until it tears itself free, leaving behind the sting and parts of its body. The injury is always fatal to the bee."

When I read that fact, I thought how it resembles what happens to us when we respond angrily and hurtfully to those who have wronged us. We *can* hurt them back. We can sting them with angry words and hurtful actions. But in the end, we probably do more damage to ourselves than we inflict upon them, especially when we consider whether or not our behavior was Christlike. What sadness we feel when we realize once again that we have failed to measure up. We bow our heads and ask the Savior to do for us what we've been unable to do for others: forgive us.

And once again he extends his honey-sweet gift of grace to us—and urges us to share it.

5

Continual Praise,
Contagious Joy

Count it all joy when you fall into various trials, know-
ing that the testing of your faith produces patience.

—JAMES 1:2–3

D uring those stressful days as our daughter Vikki neared the end of her difficult pregnancy, my cell phone went on the blink. Isn't that just like one of those whiz-bang space-age gadgets to die when you should be depending on it most urgently? With all that was going on, I *had* to have a working cell phone. I couldn't bear the thought that Vikki might need me and be unable to reach me.

Someone took it back to the phone store for me to get

it checked out, but it couldn't be repaired. So this kind person bought me a new phone—but didn't get it activated because I had pictures stored on the old phone that I wanted to keep, and in order to keep them they had to be downloaded to a computer and then reloaded onto the new phone. No one had time to do that downloading and reloading; we were all overloaded with too many other loads!

Finally, the next day, I attempted the task, but nothing would work. The pictures wouldn't copy. We even took the phone back to the store and asked the technician to try it, but he had no success either. After two frustrating days, I made an executive decision: I threw away the old phone, photos and all, so I could get the new phone activated. Whew! What a relief it was to just move on and put an end to the lost time, lost pictures, lost calls, maybe lost business. (And possibly a few lost friends. Believe it or not, I tend to get cranky when a technical gadget refuses to cooperate, and since the gadget doesn't care what kind of mood I'm in, I sometimes "download" my feelings on whoever happens to be standing nearby.)

I had a new cell phone that worked. But the relief didn't last long.

The next day, a Thursday, I flew to Detroit for a Women of Faith conference, and as I walked out of the house, I picked up my husband's cell phone charger instead of mine. I spent so much time talking on the phone in the airports and during the cab ride in Detroit that the phone was dead by the time I got to the hotel. As soon as I realized I'd brought the wrong charger, my wonderful assistant, Pat, who never breaks or loses or picks up the wrong anything, called home and arranged for the right charger to be shipped to me overnight. Finally, Friday afternoon, I could charge up my cell phone and keep in touch with Vikki and my grandchild-to-be back in Texas. Everything was rosy.

Until Saturday.

Would you believe, when I headed out to the arena Saturday morning, I walked right out of the hotel room and left that cell phone behind!? So, after all I'd been through to make sure I stayed in touch with my family while I was away, I went through the entire conference on Saturday without a phone and without a clue about how Vikki was doing. And, I might add, without a shred of patience with myself for being so addle-brained.

By any chance are you smiling? Have you ever had one of those weeks when things start out wrong and just keep on going, and you get increasingly frustrated, aggravated, agitated, irritated, and all those other "*a*-teds"?

Now let me ask you this: did it make a good story? Did you share it with your family and friends and make them smile? (It's always easier to laugh at someone else's "*a*-teds" rather than your own, isn't it?) Isn't it a relief to finally get through some ongoing trial and be able to look back on it and laugh?

I'm just guessing, but the apostle James was probably talking about a more serious trial than an uncooperative cell phone (and a forgetful mind) when he wrote that we're to "count it all joy." But I can tell you for sure that a joyful attitude sure makes trials easier to bear, no matter how trivial or terrible the trial is. Added to the Romans 8:28 promise that the Lord makes "all things work together for good to those who love God," it's easy to see that our Creator expects us to cling to our faith and keep a positive mind-set, no matter what kind of problems we're facing.

You know, we Christians aren't like other folks. Even when the hardest thing happens to us, when serious illness incapacitates us or death claims those who are dearest to us, we're comforted by God's loving presence with us in our grief and by his steadfast promises that we'll be together again someday in heaven with our departed loves ones. So even though we mourn their passing, we don't "grieve like the rest of men, who have no hope" (1 Thessalonians 4:13 NIV).

The Oil of Joy, the Garment of Praise

The Old Testament prophet Isaiah said he had been anointed by "the Spirit of the Lord GOD . . . to comfort all who mourn, to console those who mourn . . . , to give them beauty for ashes, the oil of joy for mourning, the garment of praise for the spirit of heaviness" (Isaiah 61:1–3). And let me tell you, when I'm mired down in misery, it's that "oil of joy" and "garment of praise" I crave most.

Whatever you're enduring right now, meditate on that passage and feel the Spirit of the Lord God anointing you with the oil of joy and clothing you with the garment of praise. God wants you to know he's there with you, whatever you're facing. And even if you're doing OK right now, he wants to be an encouraging, joyful part of your "normal" existence. Romans 12:1 says, "Take your everyday, ordinary life—your sleeping, eating, going-to-work, and walking-around life—and place it before God as an offering. Embracing what God does for you is the best thing you can do for him" (MSG).

Sister, God is in the extreme makeover business!

Embrace the gifts he offers: beauty for the ashes of your heartache, the oil of joy for your mourning, and a garment of praise for your spirit of heaviness. Let those gifts make over your sour attitude, your downcast expression, and your sorrow-filled ways and turn you into a "new creation," as promised in 2 Corinthians 5:17. And remember, this God-inspired makeover doesn't happen just once. It's a gift we can claim daily. The writer of Lamentations said, "Because of the LORD's great love we are not consumed, for his compassions never fail. They are new every morning; great is your faithfulness" (3:22–23 NIV).

Have you ever offered someone a gift only to have him or her refuse it? (Frankly, that happens to me quite often. I offer my friends and family the gift of my opinion, and they just go right on, ignoring the marvelous wisdom I have to share.) One time I looked high and low to get just the right shoelaces my granddaughter Vanessa had been wanting. But when I proudly delivered them to her, expecting her face to light up, she shook her head and sadly handed them back. "Grammy, those aren't the right ones," she said. I was crushed.

And after Hurricane Katrina swept ashore last year and heartbreaking reports were made of hospitals in a hopeless and helpless state and people dying because they were cut off from medical help, I heard on the news that Fidel Castro offered to send a thousand physicians from Cuba to help. The United States did accept help from other nations, but to Cuba we said no. We're not on good terms with that country, and we refused the gift it offered.

Whether it's intended that way or not, refusing a gift is an insult, a hurt, to the giver. So when God offers us these gifts to transform our minds and shift our attitudes from sorrow or criticism to joy and happiness, I suspect it hurts his feelings when we refuse them. And surely none of us wants to hurt our loving Father.

But just how does it work, this miraculous makeover? Well, one way is to put on that garment of praise *first* and let it work its goodness in you. When popular recording artist Tammy Trent's husband failed to surface from the Blue Lagoon in Jamaica, where he had gone free diving, Tammy anxiously paced the docks, watching for him. She asked some boaters to drive her around the lagoon to look for Trent. Then divers were called in, and she found herself alone in the back room of a restaurant, waiting, praying, and hoping.

Amazingly, during that agonizing time, the next thing she instinctively did was to lift her voice in praise to the Lord, singing the worship songs she'd sung all her life.

The songs didn't bring Trent back. They didn't suddenly take Tammy's tears away. But they helped her get through the crisis and, later, to endure Trent's death. Now Tammy's still singing praise songs to the Lord at Women of Faith and Revolve conferences around the country, and at other venues as well, and her story shows how praising God can help us find joy again when life's harshest realities are thrown at us.

Do you remember that old, traditional song that says, "If you're happy and you know it, then your life will surely show it"? That should be a theme song for Christians everywhere! We can be joyful in a broken world, and we know it—because we know Jesus. And we know where we're goin' when this life is over. Sure, we'll have dark days and temporary setbacks, but the Bible tells us "our light and momentary troubles are achieving for us an eternal glory that far outweighs them all" (2 Corinthians 4:17 NIV). Now, that's something to praise God about!

Here's the long and short of it, sister: we're admonished to praise God in good times and bad, to praise him with everything we have, to honor him with singing and dance just like Tammy Trent does today. We're to clap our hands, stomp our feet, and shout hurrah so we show the world the joy we find in the Lord. Except for the few people we may scare off by our wild exaltations, that kind of joy is contagious. It's infectious. It's impossible to resist. Even God himself is drawn to us when we praise him with all our being—and then he joins in the praises himself! Zephaniah 3:14–17 says:

> Sing, O daughter of Zion; shout aloud, O Israel! Be glad and rejoice with all your heart, O daughter of Jerusalem! For the LORD will remove his hand of judgment and will disperse the armies of your enemy. And the LORD himself, the King of Israel, will live among you! At last your troubles will be over, and you will fear disaster no more.
>
> On that day the announcement to Jerusalem will be, "Cheer up, Zion! Don't be afraid! For the LORD your God has arrived to live among you. He is a mighty savior. He will rejoice over you with great gladness. With his love, he will calm all your fears. He will exult over you by singing a happy song." (NLT)

Oh, my goodness! Can you imagine God—the Creator of the world—exulting over *you*? Can you even imagine that when you sing praises to God, *he sings back to you*?

To be honest, it's almost too much for my poor little

mind to grasp. But I know with all my heart that when I sing praises to God, something is happening in heaven, because my spirit gets relief, my emotions change from negative to positive, my mind feels inspired to think more wisely, my heart is guarded from the pain I might otherwise experience, my physical body relaxes, and I'm drawn into his presence knowing his loving arms are wrapped around me in his safe and secure protection.

Other than that . . . nothin' much happens. (Sorry. That was a joke—just some of that praise-produced joy bubblin' up out of me when I praise the Lord God Almighty.)

Praising God as a Way of Life

Make a habit of praising God throughout your day and just see if it doesn't soothe your spirit's dryness with the oil of joy. Don't make it a one-time morning or bedtime deal. And don't wait until you get an answer to your prayers or a blessing from God before you praise him. God is good all the time, and we need to praise him all the time—whether or not we feel like it!

I watched my Granny praise God continually—even during hard times. In fact, I didn't realize until later just how horrendous things were for her because she always had an attitude of praise for God no matter what her circumstances were, and that praise gave her a joyful attitude. When someone's always singing praises, it's hard to remember—or to realize in the first place—that his or her life may not be a bowl of cherries. While we're praising God, it's hard for us to remember our own problems! In the midst of Granny's problems, she would always say, "We praise him in the morning, praise him in the noonday, praise him all night long. Whether we want to or not, whether we feel like it or not, we praise him. It doesn't matter how we feel; it matters how we praise."

That strong directive stuck in my mind and gave me a foundation to build from during my own hard times. Remembering Granny's strong advice, I too developed an attitude of praise. I saw Granny praising God while she knelt on her knees beside her bed but also while she was bending over the ironing board, working in the kitchen, worshiping in church, walking down the street, talking on the phone, combing her hair (or mine), getting dressed, going to bed. Praising God was a way of life for her. If she was singing a song while she peeled potatoes, it was a praise song. If she was saying a prayer as she folded the laundry, it was a prayer of praise and thankfulness.

How blessed I am that Granny passed that legacy

down to me. Today, praising God is one of my favorite activities. When people ask me what my favorite pastime is, I boldly answer, "Praising God, loving on God—that's my favorite thing to do."

The reactions I get vary widely. Sometimes people think I'm being funny. And sometimes I get strange looks of disgust or pity. But that's all right. I don't need anyone else's approval or cooperation. I just go right on praising God and glorifying his name in the morning, in the noonday, and all night long, just like Granny said.

God loves to be praised. In fact he created us so we could glorify him. The Bible is full of songs of praise, stories of praise, and instructions to praise. And while God's children have praised him throughout the ages for all the wonderful things he has done and all the blessings he has bestowed, we also need to praise him without asking him for anything and praise him without even thanking him for anything. We just need to praise him for *who he is*: our magnificent Father, the Creator of the universe. Here are some scriptural examples to get you started:

"O my Strength, I sing praise to you; you, O God, are my fortress, my loving God" (Psalm 59:17 NIV).

"Let them praise the name of the LORD, for his name alone is exalted; his splendor is above the earth and the heavens" (Psalm 148:13 NIV).

"Praise the LORD, O my soul. O LORD my God, you are very great; you are clothed with splendor and majesty" (Psalm 104:1 NIV).

"You are awesome, O God, in your sanctuary; the God of Israel gives power and strength to his people. Praise be to God!" (Psalm 68:35 NIV).

"My mouth is filled with your praise, declaring your splendor all day long" (Psalm 71:8 NIV).

"Sing to God, sing praise to his name, extol him who rides on the clouds—his name is the LORD—and rejoice before him. A father to the fatherless, a

defender of widows, is God in his holy dwelling"
(Psalm 68:4–5 NIV).

"Blessed be your glorious name, and may it be
exalted above all blessing and praise. You alone are the
LORD. You made the heavens, even the highest heavens, and all their starry host, the earth and all that is
on it, the seas and all that is in them. You give life to
everything, and the multitudes of heaven worship you"
(Nehemiah 9:5–6 NIV).

Are you getting the idea? God loves to hear our
praise. And as we express it, our focus turns upward,
away from ourselves and our problems. Praising God
changes us. As we lift our hearts and minds to
praise God, we also feel that praise showering
down over us, lifting our spirits, oiling us with joy,
and intersecting with our problems and difficulties.

Godly praise is like the extra pollen that covers a
bee as it burrows into a blossom in search of nectar or
pollen to take back to the hive. When the pollen-
covered bee lands on another flower, some of that

extra pollen rubs off, causing the flower to be fertilized and its future to be confirmed. In the same way, your joyful praise for God is bound to rub off on those around you—just like Granny's praise-filled attitude rubbed off on me.

When I awaken each morning, my first thought is to think praises to God. You may think I'm exaggerating, but I'm not. While I'm washing my face, brushing my teeth, taking my bath, putting on my clothes, I'm in praise mode. Some of my most powerful praise times are during my morning "getting ready" time.

I'll always remember one wonderful Sunday morning when I was bathing and listening to a CD that includes a praise song that always makes me want to dance. I was in such an attitude of praise that I ended up dancing around the bedroom wearing nothing but a towel—and it was more of an accessory than an item of apparel, if you know what I mean! My husband was at the other end of the house where I didn't think he could hear me singing along with the CD. But he happened to walk into the room and was startled to see me dancing over the carpet in that state of undress! Before I knew it, we were both dancing and praising the Lord together. Psalm 149:3 says, "Let them praise his name with dancing" (NIV), and that's exactly what we were doing—which was something to praise God for in itself, because my husband and I hadn't danced together for many years. What a joyful morning that was—and what a joy-filled memory it is today. Are you getting the message? If you want to be a joyful person, if you want to have the kind of joy that other people can "catch," then begin by praising.

The only thing better than praising God is . . . praising God with other people. That's why I sometimes invite as many as fifty or sixty friends and women in Daughters of Zion, my mentoring ministry, to weekend retreats that include pajama praise parties. We gather in a hotel somewhere and spend the weekend in workshops and worship sessions. Then, at about 10 p.m., we meet in a hotel ballroom, wearing our robes and sleepwear, for that late-night pajama praise party. (I'm careful to tell the girls this is a *pajama* party, not a *lingerie* party!) A talented leader directs us in a free-flowing, exuberant, unstructured time of loving the Lord and singing his praises. We go at it every way we know how until 3 a.m. It's an experience you would expect to be exhausting, but instead it's energizing.

When Normal Words Don't Work

If you've ever been to a praise and worship service, you know it usually starts with uplifting, blow-the-roof-off music that lifts your focus totally onto our awesome, all-powerful God. You just can't hear that kind of music without being swept up in a rush of joy as you praise the God of creation. Thinking about the effect this music has on so many of us, I started wondering what might have prompted people in biblical times to instinctively glorify the Lord. Often something happened that caused even nonbelievers to burst into spontaneous praise for God.

For example, the Old Testament tells the amazing story of how King Nebuchadnezzar had three godly men, Shadrach, Meshach, and Abednego, tied up and thrown into a fiery furnace because they refused to bow down and worship his idols. Waiting in front of the flames to watch the three condemned men burn, the king was astonished to see *four* men walking, unbound, within the fire. Dumbfounded, he called for Shadrach, Meshach, and Abednego to come out of the furnace, and when they did, their hair wasn't even singed. Instead of asking a bunch of questions, the king immediately shouted out, "Praise be to the God of Shadrach, Meshach and Abednego, who has sent his angel and rescued his servants!" (Daniel 3:28 NIV).

In another story depicting instinctive praise for God, a righteous and devout man named Simeon, who lived in Jerusalem, had been told by the Holy Spirit that he would not die until he had seen the Messiah. We don't know how Simeon expected the Messiah's arrival; maybe he pictured a mighty conqueror riding into town on a magnificent chariot. Surely he was unprepared for it to happen that day in the temple when a young couple brought in a baby so that Simeon could perform a religious custom.

Simeon took the unknown baby into his arms—and promptly burst into praise for God. You see, the parents were Mary and Joseph, and that little baby boy was Jesus. Old Simeon didn't start yelling, "It's him! It's the Messiah!" Instead, he "took him in his arms and praised God" (Luke 2:28 NIV).

When Jesus grew up and began his ministry, he performed miracles throughout the land—healing the sick, casting out demons, giving sight to the blind. Now, if this happened today, we might expect people who witnessed such events to reach for their cell phones and call the newspapers or to whip out their video cameras and try to get some footage they could sell to the TV networks. Maybe modern-day folks would stand around with their mouths hanging open without a clue how such a thing could happen.

But in story after story in the New Testament, we're told that either the healed person or the crowds who witnessed the healing—or both—*immediately praised God.* Matthew 15:31 says, "The people were amazed when they saw the mute speaking, the crippled made well, the lame walk and the blind seeing. And they praised the God of Israel" (NIV).

When Jesus told a paralyzed man, "Get up, take your mat and go home," the man did just that. The crowd of people who saw this happen "were filled with awe; and they praised God" (Matthew 9:6, 8 NIV).

A woman who had been "crippled by a spirit" for eighteen years "was bent over and could not straighten up at all." Then Jesus spoke to her. "He put his hands on her, and immediately she straightened up and praised God" (Luke 13:11, 13 NIV).

And then there was the Roman centurion assigned to the execution detail on the day of Jesus's crucifixion. As Jesus breathed his last breath, others at the scene "beat their breasts and went away." But the centurion stood at the foot of the cross and, "seeing what had happened, praised God" (Luke 23:47–48 NIV).

Inspiring Others to Praise God and Catch Our Joy

Now it's our turn. By our actions and examples, by the way we love and praise and serve the Lord, we can inspire others to praise God too. Jesus said, "Let your light shine before men, that they may see your good deeds and praise your Father in heaven" (Matthew 5:16 NIV). The apostle Paul said people "praised God because of me" when they heard a report that Paul, "the man who formerly persecuted [the new Christians] is now preaching the faith he once tried to destroy" (Galatians 1:23–24 NIV). Later, when Paul asked the Corinthians for help, he said that because of their gifts "men will praise God for the obedience that accompanies your confession of the gospel of Christ, and for your generosity in sharing with them and with everyone else" (2 Corinthians 9:13 NIV). And the apostle Peter said, "If anyone speaks, he should do it as one speaking the very words of God. If anyone serves, he should do it with the strength God provides, so that in all things God may be praised through Jesus Christ. To him be the glory and the power for ever and ever. Amen" (1 Peter 4:11 NIV).

Praising God soothes *us* as it glorifies *him*. As I have increased my practice of praise, I have become more content, more confident, and more joyful in my everyday life. I'm able to relax more easily, knowing the glorious, all-powerful, majestic God who created the universe cares about me, watches over me, and is preparing a place for me. And that part about his exulting over me—well, that still seems too good to be true!

And what do you know? My relaxed and joyful state is much more appealing to my family and the people who have to work with me. As they've seen the continual praise I live, they've caught the contagious attitude it brings. Ask them, and I think they'll tell you that the atmosphere of my home and office is infused with the fragrance of joy.

Are *you* inspiring people to praise God and share the joy that comes from it?

Gettin' through the Meantime

O our God, . . . we do not know what to do, but our eyes are upon you.

—2 Chronicles 20:12 NIV

*T*his will probably come as a shock to most of you, but I am not a very patient person. I hate to wait! Of all the jobs and responsibilities and activities I have going on, the hardest things I do are wait for a doctor's appointment or wait for an overdue airplane or even wait for my nail polish to dry. Honey, I have places to go, things to do, and work to finish: office work, computer work, and housework; deadlines, standing in lines, and drawing the line when my grandchildren get too rambunctious;

washing, ironing, wearing, and washing again; shuffling papers, putting papers away, and looking for papers I can't remember where I put.

You know what I'm talking about. You're probably just as busy as I am. I may have a ton of errands to run, a long list of groceries to buy, and a computer full of e-mail that needs to be answered. But there I sit (or stand), pursing my lips, tapping my toes, heaving loud sighs, and grimacing at the clock while the receptionist or the gate agent or the guy at the deli counter calls every name or number but mine. A lot of times when my doctor is running late, I suspect my blood pressure was just fine when I arrived at his office, but by the time I finally get to an exam room, it's so high the nurse is about ready to call 911.

When I'm stuck in a place where all I can do is wait and watch the clock, I get upset. I'll tell you the truth, girlfriend: sometimes *time* just ticks me off!

Do you know what time it is when you have to wait and wait and wait some more? Can you guess what time it is when your life is put on hold while some big problem or crisis swirls around you? Any idea what time it is when something's got you living on pins and needles and you feel like you've been holding your breath for a couple of months?

That's the *mean*time, sister. And it's the hardest time

there is, especially for those of us who are always in a hurry anyway. But listen up, honey. I've learned a few lessons about getting through the meantime, and in this chapter I'm gonna share what I know.

Outmaneuvering the Meantime

One reason the meantime is so difficult for us is that we usually have no control over it. There's nothing *we* can do on our own to turn the meantime into good time. Realistically, without using terrorist tactics, we can't force the receptionist to call our name when the doctor is tied up with other patients or has been called away for an emergency. We can't force the deli clerk to slice the meat and cheese faster for the customers ahead of us. We can't snap our fingers and magically make the teenager who's out past curfew suddenly appear in the driveway. We can't squeeze a loved one's hand and bring her out of the coma.

We just have to wait. And waiting is *so* hard.

Change Your Attitude

If you're one who, like me, tends to get impatient when you're forced to wait and wait and wait, consider changing your *maditude* to *gratitude*. Instead of fretting about the time you're wasting and all the things you have to do, take advantage of the break you've been given.

Close your eyes and pray, "Thank you, Lord, for giving me this time to rest. I'm overwhelmed with all the things I *have* to do and all the things I *want* to do, and I know I don't have time for all of them. Help me to shift my focus away from those long lists of have-to-dos and want-to-dos. Please plant a little sweet-pea flower of peace in my mind right now, and help me imagine it slowly sprouting and flowering, entwining my weary spirit like a fragrant vine growing up the trellis by the porch swing. Put me there now, Lord; help me see myself relaxing in that old porch swing on a cool summer's evening, enjoying the beautiful blessing of your creation surrounding me. Thank you, Lord. I praise you, Lord. Amen."

If you're not a porch-swing person, ask Jesus to give you an image of your own favorite relaxing place where you can mentally and physically take a break and step back from the hustle-bustle world.

Recite Soothing Scripture

When I was growing up in my great-grandparents' house, Daddy Harrell taught me to use two beloved passages of Scripture to soothe my nerves and give me peace, even in the most stressful situations. Throughout my life, the Twenty-third Psalm and the Lord's Prayer have worked like spiritual Valium for me, taking the edge off my edginess and helping me grow more gracious and patient.

Since then I've stored up a mental filing cabinet full of remedial Scripture passages. Seven of my favorites are shared in my book *The Buzz*. As I said there, I've whispered memorized Scripture passages to myself as I've "waited for the phone to ring, waited for a child to come home, waited for a decision to be made, or waited for the turbulence to end at thirty thousand feet." And still today, whenever I recite them, whatever the setting, I can feel my worry easing, my blood pressure dropping, and my muscles relaxing.

Try it for yourself the next time you feel your nerves fraying and your patience falling. Prepare ahead of time by memorizing Philippians 4:6–7. Here's how I like to say it: "*BEE* anxious for *NO*-thing, but in everything by prayer and supplication, with thanksgiving, let your requests be made known to God; and the PEACE of God, which surpasses *allllllll* understanding, will guard your hearts and minds through Christ Jesus." Then, when the meantime hits, take in a breath, close your eyes, and let out the breath slowly as you repeat the powerful words that have comforted and soothed Christ's followers for hundreds of years.

A First-Aid Kit of Scripture Passages

*H*ere are some favorite Bible verses that are good to memorize and call to mind whenever you're stuck in a meantime experience:

"I can do all things through Christ who strengthens me" (Philippians 4:13).

"I will say of the LORD, 'He is my refuge and my fortress; my God, in Him I will trust'" (Psalm 91:2).

"Trust in the LORD with all your heart, and lean not on your own understanding; in all your ways acknowledge Him, and He shall direct your paths" (Proverbs 3:5–6).

"But you, O LORD, be not far off; O You my help, hasten to my assistance" (Psalm 22:19 NASB).

"Help me, O LORD my God! Oh, save me according to Your mercy" (Psalm 109:26).

"The eternal God is your refuge, and underneath are the everlasting arms" (Deuteronomy 33:27).

"He will yet fill your mouth with laughter and your lips with shouts of joy" (Job 8:21 NIV).

Fight the Overwhelming with the Underwhelming

One day I sat down at my desk and looked with dismay over the stacks and piles and boxes and heaps of papers and things I needed to tend to. The crush of stuff was overwhelming. I sat there looking at it and thought, *This ain't gonna work. I'm never gonna get all this stuff done in time to go out of town tomorrow.*

I sat there awhile longer, unable to do anything but stare at the stacks. The task just seemed too big, the time too short, my motivation too weak. I couldn't do it. I got up and walked away.

Time went by—*mean*time, it was too—as I moped

and dodged and procrastinated throughout the morning. I just did not want to go back in there and face that mess again. More meantime passed. Finally, after lunch I forced myself to return. And wouldn't you know? Those piles of papers seemed to have grown bigger!

Then the lightbulb went on in my head—I guess I finally found the switch after groping around for it all morning—and I remembered that little technique I read about somewhere. It's the KISS method for conquering paperwork: **k**eep **i**t **s**imple, **s**ugar (well, that's my version of it anyway).

I looked at those papers and thought, *Hmmmm. Keep it simple. OK.*

The method tells you to pick up one thing and either act on it or throw it away. Don't you put that thing back down and move on to the next one. No, ma'am. You either act on it (file it, respond to it, make a call about it, whatever) and/or you throw it away. *Then* you can pick up the next thing.

I took a deep breath. *OK, sugar, here we go.* I picked up the first piece of paper and was relieved to discover it needed no action. I tossed it. I picked up the next piece, jotted a reply at the bottom of it, folded it up into an envelope, stuck a stamp on it, and put it in the outer pocket of my purse to be mailed.

Well, after just two pieces of paper, I was on a roll. I was inspired. I was getting things done, baby!

Of course the KISS method didn't work flawlessly. The phone rang, the computer nagged me that I had messages waiting, my assistant popped in to ask me questions, and in a little while I got up to get some water. But I was no longer frustrated because I had begun the process, I had made a start, and I could actually see some results. My desktop was getting emptier, and my trash can was getting fuller. I loved it!

When you're stuck out there in the meantime because you dread an overwhelming task, take one small action toward getting it done. Like the old adage says, the journey of a thousand miles begins with one small step—and so do a lot of other things. You can do it. Break out of your meantime and make a start. Keep it simple, sugar, and kiss your meantime good-bye.

Let God Carry You

One evening in 1996, after our family had gathered for a fish fry, I spilled some hot grease on my arm while I was cleaning up the kitchen. The big pot just slipped out of my hand, and the grease splashed all over my arm. I had a bad, bad burn, and the pain was nearly unbearable. My family finally convinced me I needed to go to the hospital, but when we got to the ER, the staff just packed my swollen and blistered arm in ice for two hours and sent me home. They really didn't tell me how to care for my injury, and I was in too much misery to ask. I just wanted to get back home and rest.

I had to travel to a speaking engagement the next day, and I was really upset when I got to the gate and found out that the plane was full and the only seat available for me was a *middle* seat. Well, as Patsy Clairmont says, I don't *do* middle seats, honey. But the gate agent told me the same thing another gate agent had told Patsy years earlier. Either I sat in the middle seat—or out on the wing somewhere. In other words, I was sitting in that middle seat or I wasn't going!

I had wrapped my arm in layers of gauze and adhesive tape, and it had been throbbing all night and still continued to radiate excruciating pain. And let me tell you, honey, when you're in pain, that's a *real mean mean*time.

Fearful that the man in the next seat would bump it, I kept my bandaged arm tucked up against me and didn't use the armrest. As the flight took off, I leaned my head against the seat back, closed my eyes, and began my *mean*time litany, silently reciting the Lord's Prayer, the Twenty-third Psalm, and Philippians 4:6–7.

I sensed my seatmate moving in his seat and opened my eyes to find that he had turned toward me and had his eyes focused on my bandages. "Let me see your arm," he said rather abruptly.

I was a little shocked that he would say such a thing without even introducing himself or saying hello or making any kind of chitchat.

"Oh no, sir. My arm is throbbing. I burned it, and it really hurts," I answered.

"Let me see it," he insisted.

I couldn't believe he was talking to me that way. I shook my head no.

Finally his voice softened, and he realized he hadn't explained himself.

"I'm sorry," he said. "I'm a doctor. Maybe I could offer some suggestions."

When he said that, I smiled. Isn't God awesome? I smiled and sent up a silent prayer: *OK, Lord, I get it. That's why I'm sitting in this particular middle seat.*

I unwrapped the messy, stained gauze from my arm. The doctor's eyebrows shot up when he saw the fiery-red, blistered skin. "Do you know how to take care of it?" he said.

I shook my head. "Not really."

"This is what you have to do," he began. "You *have* to do this; do you understand?"

I nodded.

"Every day, twice a day, you wash your arm, and you get all the dead skin off—all of it—every day. You have to scrub it, and it will hurt. But if you'll do that, you'll be much less likely to have an infection and be left with a terrible scar."

Those instructions began one of the meanest mean-time rituals I've ever experienced, but I did what the doctor said. Every day, twice a day, I scrubbed my arm with Dial soap until the dead skin was all rubbed off. Then I ran cold water over it, trying unsuccessfully to ease the pain. As I washed, I recited the Twenty-third Psalm in between wiping away tears and sobbing out my agony.

Even though I was in bad shape, I had to keep working and fulfilling my national speaking obligations. I was faithfully washing my burned arm every day as the doctor had instructed me. But what no one had told me was that I also needed to drink lots of water to avoid getting dehydrated. Burned flesh consumes a lot of moisture, and that moisture needs to be replaced.

A few days later I was in Orlando to present a speech. I was so ill I could barely stagger down the hall to the room where the group had gathered. A hotel staff member saw me holding on to the wall as I walked, took one look at my face masked in misery, and asked if he could call the paramedics. I refused. I was determined to fulfill my obligation and give that speech! But the minute I finished and turned to step down from the podium, I swayed awkwardly, almost falling. In fact, I would have fallen right off the platform if the hotel manager hadn't been there waiting for me. The staff member, who had seen me staggering down the hall had told him I was in trouble, and he had taken matters into his own hands. "Ma'am, we have a car waiting for you," he said. "You *are* going to the hospital."

That time I was smart enough not to argue. I hardly remember the trip to the emergency room or anything that happened to me there. Later a nurse told me I was so severely dehydrated they had trouble getting an IV started.

The emergency room staff got me stabilized enough that I could travel, and the next day I flew back to Dallas, where my husband met my flight and took me straight to Parkland Hospital. Although I was terribly sick and weakened by the dehydration, my burned arm was doing remarkably well. In fact, the medical staff members were surprised when they saw it.

"Who did this? Who cleaned your arm for you?" one of them asked.

Knowing how painful the scrubbing can be, they could hardly believe I'd done it myself. In fact, one staff member thought I'd done such a good job, he asked me if I would come to work there as a burn scrubber! I didn't even have to think one split second about how to answer: no way!

When I look back on that horrible experience, that miserable meantime, I ask myself how I got through it. There is no other answer but the grace of God; in his great mercy, God gave me the strength and endurance to stand over those sinks—at home and in hotel rooms around the country—and scrub off that skin. Sometimes, sister, there are meantimes that are so mean only God himself can get you through, and that was one of those times for me. There was only one set of footprints behind me after I passed over that meantime beach, and they weren't mine.

When you're stuck in a hard time, when life has burned you and left you lying in a heap, grasp the grace of God, let his everlasting arms lift you spiritually and emotionally until you can do what must be done. Let the powerful words of memorized Scripture passages flow through your mind. And for heaven's sake, find yourself a good professional who will tell you *everything* you need to know about dealing with your meantime problem!

Don't Pray for Patience!

A Sunday school teacher once said she'd told herself she would never, ever pray for patience again. "Every time I've asked God to help me learn to be more patient, he's helped me learn, all right. But I've had to learn the hard way! I pray for patience, and the next thing I know I'm in some long, torturous ordeal with no way out of it and just one way through it. The only choice I have is to force myself to be patient—or lose my mind."

The teacher was joking; in that same lesson she urged us to live a Christlike life, and Jesus was infinitely patient. But there *was* some truth in what she said. Remember that verse that started off chapter 5? "Count it all joy when you fall into various trials, knowing that *the testing of your faith produces patience*" (James 1:2–3, emphasis mine). And then there's that next verse in the first chapter of James: "But let patience have its perfect work, that you may be perfect and complete, lacking nothing."

With all the meantime experiences I've had in being patient, I figure I must be just about perfect by now!

No Such Thing
as Failure

The stone which the builders rejected
Has become the chief cornerstone.
This was the LORD's doing;
It is marvelous in our eyes.

—Psalm 118:22–23

I've made some mistakes in my life. In fact, I've made some whoppers. For instance, when I worked as a bank officer, I would leave my banking job in the evening, dash home to change clothes, and then head out to teach a banking class, deliver a speech somewhere, or attend a board meeting. Maybe I enjoyed being on "important" boards just because I liked to see my name on the fancy corporate letterhead.

One night when our youngest child, Lesa, was fourteen

and was our only child still living at home, I was rushing out to attend yet another meeting when she stopped me at the door. "Mama, wait a minute," she said. "I need to talk to you."

"What is it, honey?" I said impatiently. "I'm in a hurry."

Lesa stood in front of me and looked me in the eye. "Mama, are you ever going to be home for anything I'm doing?"

I probably stood there a full minute, staring back at her with that telltale guilty-as-charged, deer-in-the-headlights look. Lord, have mercy! Was I that bad? Had I forgotten that I had a teenage daughter who needed me? Was it possible that her good father was not a good mother too?

I drove off to my meeting, feeling as though a big ol' knife had been plunged into my heart. I was sure I had failed as a mother. What kind of parent would get so busy with other people and other issues that she didn't notice the little miracle she, her husband, and God had created, standing hopefully by the door, watching longingly through the window night after night, hoping her mother would pause long enough in her comings and goings to see that the child needed motherly attention?

I not only *felt* like a failure at that moment, I guess I *was* a failure, because I went right on to my meeting, wiping away tears as I drove. On my way, the words of Romans 8:28 came to my mind: "And we know that all things work together for good to those who love God, to those who are the called according to His purpose."

That's when I started praying. (Since we're not supposed to talk on our cell phones when we're driving, isn't it wonderful that we can call heaven without needing any kind of technical gadget? And these days, I feel even more fortunate because when other drivers see me alone in my car, earnestly talking and waving my hands, they no longer think I'm a crazy woman. They just think I'm using a hands-free device.)

I said, "Lord, I know *you* can make all things work together for good, so I know you can take my failure—my major mothering malfunction—and turn it into something wonderful. But, dear Father, would you give *me* a second chance to make things better? Would you let me get back home safely tonight so I can fix the mess I've made—and would you please help me do it? Guide me in making better choices, empower me to say no when some big corporation offers to put my name on its fancy letterhead, and, dear Jesus, help me remember that *you* are my first priority and my family is second, and waaaaaaaay down the list are those businesspeople who say they need

my advice and hope for my support and want my partici-
pation. Thank you, God, for being a much better parent
than I am. Help me be more like you. Amen."

OK, so that's not *exactly* what I said. I've had several
years to edit my remarks! But that was the gist of my
prayer that night—and no matter what words I used, my
Father knew what I needed.

You know, a lot of times we rush off to tend to a misguided priority and something happens so that we don't
get another opportunity to make things right. The way
folks drive in Dallas (and anywhere else, for that matter),
I could have backed out of my driveway that night and
been killed by a distracted motorist, or I could have been
crushed by an out-of-control semi on the freeway. Instead,
I made it through that night's event, vowing to myself the
whole time that the very next day I would start making
changes so I could spend more time with my child—and
with my husband too.

A Second Chance to Make Things Right . . .
and a Third . . .

I'm so grateful for every second chance God has
granted me, especially the one he gave me to fix things

with my family. The way I see it, if we can manage to live through a failure, then it's not a failure; it's the first step in a valuable learning experience. God has such a marvelous and miraculous way of selecting those of us who seem the unlikeliest to succeed or are the most miserable misfits and using us for his glory. If you don't believe me, just look at the genealogy of Jesus recorded in the first chapter of the Gospel of Matthew. Girl, there are some real scoundrels in that list! But God touched the lives of those Old Testament "failures" and gave them a second chance to make things right. They seized that opportunity, and as a result, they became the ancestors of the Messiah whose names open the New Testament.

One of those ancestors is described in a story told in 1 Samuel 16. The prophet Samuel was sent to the house of Jesse to anoint the one who would be the next king of Israel. God told Samuel he would tell him when the next king stood before him. One by one, seven of Jesse's sons were brought in. They were strong, capable men, and as each one stood before him, Samuel felt certain *this* would be the one. But each time Samuel was wrong. He was confused by what was happening, but God told him, "The LORD does not look at the things man looks at. Man looks at the outward appearance, but the LORD looks at the heart" (v. 7 NIV).

After the seven sons were all rejected as the next king, Samuel asked Jesse, "Are these all the sons you have?"

"There is still the youngest," Jesse answered, "but he is tending the sheep."

"Send for him," Samuel said. (See verse 11 NIV.)

As his seven tall, strong, older, more kingly brothers stood by, a handsome young boy was led in to stand before Samuel. And wouldn't you know? God told Samuel, "Rise and anoint him; he is the one" (v. 12 NIV).

Did I mention the boy's name? David.

And consider the apostle Paul, whose story is told in the New Testament and who is known to us today as one of the greatest of Jesus's followers. Over the last two thousand years, his letters to the early churches have become blueprints for generations of Christians, showing us how we're to live our lives and serve our Savior. But before Paul became one of the most passionate of Christ's followers, he was their greatest persecutor, devising every way imaginable to torture and kill them.

Then Jesus touched his life, and Paul came to understand that we serve a gracious God who blesses us with second chances. Paul used his failure as a learning experience, writing, "Christ Jesus came into the world to save sinners—of whom I am the worst. But for that very reason

I was shown mercy so that in me, the worst of sinners, Christ Jesus might display his unlimited patience as an example for those who would believe on him and receive eternal life" (1 Timothy 1:15–16 NIV).

Jesus has "unlimited patience" to forgive us for being stupid. Or mean. Or thoughtless. Or hurtful. When we confess our failures and ask him to forgive us, he does so gladly. And then he loves to see us use our second chances to correct our mistakes and get back on the Christlike path. That's not to say it's always easy to fix the mistakes we've made. When I was trying to fix my failings as a mother, I had to think long and hard about what to give up so that I had more time with my family. But soon I resigned from most of the boards I served on as well as several professional organizations. To my amazement, those boards and groups didn't fold up and die after I left. In fact, they're all still out there today, twenty years later, humming along just fine and dandy without Ms. Thelma Wells, thank you very much. Ain't that somethin'?

A short while later I resigned from my full-time job at a bank to start my own business. The day the bank president called me into his office to say good-bye, he also gave me some great advice. He had seen the way I scurried all over the city, flitting from one meeting or class or board session to the next, and that day he told me, "Thelma, I know you're going to be a success; I have no doubts about that. But there's one thing I want you to remember: when you get too busy for your family, you're too busy. People are much more important than papers."

I took his advice to heart, and I made a lot of changes and improvements in my mothering style after going through that valuable learning experience. *Most* of the time since then, I've managed to live by what I learned. And now, although I try to be modest, the truth is, I think I'm doing an extraordinarily good job as the family matriarch. I'm still an extremely busy woman, but my family is a top priority—as shown back in chapter 3, where I described how I welcome into our home on a regular basis the whole wild, loud, boisterous tribe.

And, honey, those are just the routine Sunday dinners we share a couple of times a month. My home is also headquarters for a lot of holiday and birthday celebrations too. My daughters say they just can't celebrate their birthdays properly unless the whole family is gathered. And Vikki always wants me to make her favorite strawberry cake (the recipe is in the box on page 111). On *their* special occasions, the grandkids flock to Grammy's for my famous spaghetti and meatballs. (I'll wait until they're older to admit that the meatballs and the garlic-buttered Italian bread come frozen from the warehouse club and that Grammy's famous sauce recipe has just one line: "Heat up a jar of Ragu.")

Vikki's Favorite Strawberry Birthday Cake
(This recipe was taken from an old church cookbook.)

Ingredients (also see the frosting ingredients below):
1 box white cake mix
3 tablespoons flour
1 small box strawberry gelatin
$\frac{1}{2}$ cup water
$\frac{3}{4}$ cup oil
4 eggs
$\frac{1}{2}$ of an 8-oz. box frozen, sliced strawberries in sugar, thawed. (You'll use the rest of the strawberries in the frosting.)

Directions:
Combine the cake mix, flour, and gelatin mix. Add water and oil and mix well. Add eggs and beat 2

minutes. Stir in strawberries. Bake in a 9 x 13 pan at 350 degrees for 50–60 minutes, until a toothpick inserted into the center of the cake comes out clean.

Frosting:

1 stick margarine

1 1-lb. box powdered sugar (about 4 cups, more or less)

½ box frozen, sliced strawberries in sugar

Soften margarine; cream in the powdered sugar. Add enough strawberries to make it spreading consistency. Be careful not to put in too much liquid; you want a frosting consistency, not a sauce. Then spread it onto the cake, top with candles, sing "Happy Birthday," and share with friends and family.

Another Failure—and a Success Story

While we're talking about cooking again and I'm telling you about all the meals and good food I prepare for my family left and right, let me just confess something else I failed at while I was raising my kids:

I never taught my daughters how to cook.

That's right. Granny taught me, and I should have taught my girls. Believe me, I tried. And tried. And tried. But they weren't interested. I started off trying to teach Vikki a few things in the kitchen, and she said, "What am I going to learn that for?"

"So you can survive, baby," I told her. I'd be busy showing her how to do things, and I'd look over and she'd be sitting at the kitchen table reading a magazine. "Vikki, you are going to have to do this one day," I would say to her.

"I'll just eat out," she would answer. "Besides, Mama, I can't cook because I burn myself every time I touch the stove or go near the oven. So I can't cook."

The same thing happened with Lesa, although today she does like to bake things.

But once again, my "failure" has been turned into something good. Instead of learning to cook much of anything herself, Lesa *married* a good cook. Wasn't that smart? And before Vikki got married, she finally admitted she needed to know how to put a meal together and asked me for help.

Maybe you're thinking I smugly took her home to my kitchen, got out the cookbooks, and passed along all those wonderful cooking methods Granny taught me.

Naw, you didn't think that, did you?

I didn't teach her how Granny made things (the hard way). I took her on a field trip and taught her where to find Granny's meals, already made, in the frozen food section of the grocery store! Listen up, honey. Today we do things smarter, not harder—remember? Did you know you can buy frozen corn that's already buttered and squash that's ready to heat up and serve? There are prepared meats—roast beef, ham, and pork chops—you can heat up in your microwave and have on the table in just a few minutes that will make your family and friends think you've slaved over the stove for hours.

There are mixes and kits you can make according to the package directions or enhance a bit with other ingredients (see the box on page 115 for my doctored-up mac-and-cheese recipe). You can even buy fresh greens—turnip, mustard, collard—already washed and chopped and waiting for the cookin' pot. All you have to do is take 'em home, put 'em in the pot, add water, seasonings, and some bacon or ham hocks, and let 'em cook awhile.

Mama T's Doctored-Up Mac-and-Cheese

Honey, it's probably best that you don't tell your doctor you're eatin' this stuff, although if you eat too much of it, I suspect he'll find out sooner or later.

Ingredients:

Kraft Deluxe Macaroni & Cheese Dinner, family size (the kind that comes with the cheese sauce in a foil pouch)

pinch of salt

a pat of butter

1 regular-size can cream of mushroom soup

1 8-oz. pkg. shredded cheddar cheese

1 egg

a little milk

a little flour

1–2 more pats of butter

Directions:

Boil the pasta according to package directions. I like to add a pat of butter as it's boiling so it doesn't stick, and I put in just a pinch of salt. When the pasta's done, drain and set aside.

Empty the cheese sauce pouch into a large mixing bowl. Stir in the cream of mushroom soup, then stir in the milk—$\frac{1}{2}$ cup or less—enough to make the cheese mixture smooth and thin enough to stir. Add the egg and stir again, then add a couple of pats of butter (cut up the pats so the butter spreads throughout the mixture). Now sprinkle on just a pinch of flour—just a little, maybe a tablespoon—over the top of the cheese mixture and stir that in too.

Gently stir the pasta into the cheese mixture so that all the pasta is coated, then turn it out into a 9 x 12 or 9 x 13 pan. Sprinkle half the grated cheese on top in a thin layer. Bake in a 350-degree oven until it gets settled and looks a little hard on top, usually around 10 minutes or so. Take it out of the oven, sprinkle on the rest of the cheese, then put it back in the oven for another 5–10 minutes until that additional cheese melts. Take it out of the oven and let it sit a few minutes, then serve it up!

OK, so I do have a few pangs of guilt, imagining what Granny would say if she knew I was doing things the easy way. She might say I'd failed as a steward of my finances. Granny never wanted to pay extra for something (like washed and chopped collard greens) that she could do herself. She grew a lot of her own vegetables, and she took advantage of anything free that she could find. For example, my Aunt Doretha would ask permission to pick the crab apples off the trees in front of the bank where I worked. She would give Granny bagfuls of those crab apples, and from them Granny made the best crab-apple preserves you've ever tasted. The bankers thought of those trees as ornamental. Aunt Doretha and Granny thought of them as free provisions from God.

Granny wouldn't have done things the way I do them today. But Granny didn't travel across the country and around the world, either, sharing the gospel message and carrying God's love to those who need to feel its presence confirmed in their lives. Granny was totally devoted to serving her family and serving her God through his church. And so am I. I may have failed to follow her methods, but I've found a way to turn that "failure" into a streamlined system that lets me achieve the same goals. And she would be quick to laugh and tell me Jesus had used my "failings" to help me do something good.

And finally, let me just say, I wasn't a *total* failure in teaching my kids to cook. My girls couldn't have cared less, but it turns out that while our son, George, was growing up, sitting at the kitchen table, talking to me while I banged and clanged out a meal to feed the family, *he* paid attention! I never really taught him anything in the kitchen, but he watched and learned! Today he's a very talented cook. He's probably the one who follows Granny's lead in the kitchen more than anyone else in our family. He mixes his own blends of seasonings and comes up with his own original recipes. I'm not surprised, because even as a child he could put together a meal like you wouldn't believe—although I didn't know it at the time.

When George was around the age of twelve or thirteen, he would cook up a batch of biscuits, make his own gravy . . . and fry *squirrels* he killed with a BB gun in our backyard! He would shoot those poor squirrels, skin 'em and dress 'em, and fry 'em up like chicken. Then he and Lesa, who is six years younger than George and thinks her big brother hung the moon, would sit down for an after-school feast! This went on while I was still at work.

Granny lived with us at that time, but she was ill and didn't really know what was going on (or maybe she did know and thought it was wonderful that her great-great-grandson was so inventive!). George and Lesa would have everything cleaned up by the time I got home, so I didn't have a clue it was happening. In fact, I didn't know anything about these little kitchen capers until the kids were grown and started laughing and joking about it at one of our family gatherings. Talk about a failure turning into something good! I'm sure it must have been illegal to go "hunting" and to shoot a BB gun inside the city limits, but out of that misguided adventure, George became a clever and imaginative cook.

A Failure to Be Factual

When I finally recognized my earlier failings, I did an extreme mama makeover, and today I preside over my family's gatherings, supremely proud of myself for being such a good Mama T and Grammy. I sit there in my throne room (that would be my kitchen), surrounded by loved ones coming and going, and think, *Thelma Wells, you are one marvelous mama.*

I am living proof that our Creator can take the most

miserable failure and turn it into something fabulous. *I am that failure-turned-fabulous something!*

That's my attitude as I sit there thinking, *Yes indeed, Thelma, you are all that and a bag of chips!* (Oh, girl, I know you won't believe this, but sometimes I can get an attitude goin', and it's a wonder my head doesn't just swell up and explode. I guess I was in one of those attitudes the day I hung that sign in our garage by the door heading into the house. It says, "My husband is the king of this house . . . until the queen comes home!")

But then, while I'm sitting there thinking I'm oh so wonderful, a whiny little voice comes sneaking in from somewhere in the back of my head, back there where the orneriest brain cells live—the ones that should be remembering things like where I left my car keys, what time my doctor's appointment is, and where I'm flying to on Thursday but instead keep reminding me of all the failures I've inflicted on myself and others. And not just my ordinary first-time failures but my *repeated* failures. They're the worst kind.

What about last week when you worked on that proposal instead of calling that woman who e-mailed you, asking you to pray with her? the voice pointedly asks. *What about that day when Lesa came by?* it says accusingly.

Well! What a shock. It turns out I'm not perfect after all. I've not only failed once, I've failed too many times to count! And even worse, I *haven't* always learned from my mistakes.

When they were growing up, I taught my kids, Don't make the same mistakes everyone else makes. Learn from their example. If you're gonna make a mistake, let it be something original. If you're gonna mess up, don't make the same mess twice. If you're gonna fail, fail at something new.

Yes, ma'am, that's the lesson I taught my kids: learn from your mistakes. And then I went right out and repeated the same mistakes myself. (I rationalize that sometimes we learn from others' example, and sometimes *we* have to *be* the example for others. We take turns, right?) That's what that little voice in the back of my head reminds me every time I get to thinking Thelma Wells is too good to be true.

One of those repeated failings happened when I was overwhelmed with paperwork at my office. Lesa came by, reminding me that I had promised to go with her to take care of a financial matter. I looked at all the papers scattered all over my desk, and I looked at my daughter standing there expectantly, and, girlfriend, would you believe I chose the papers over my precious Lesa?

"Honey, I'm sorry. I just don't have time to go with you like I'd hoped," I said apologetically. "You can do it on your own. It's not hard. Just walk in there and sign the papers. There's nothing to it. You don't need me to go with you."

"But, Mama, you said you'd go," Lesa answered. "I've never done this before. I need you with me."

"Come on, Lesa. Look at this mess," I said, maybe just a little impatiently, as I waved my arm over the stacks of papers scattered over my desk. "I can't go."

Lesa let out a sigh, gave me one last, hard look, and headed out the door.

I returned to my papers, but my conscience wouldn't let me work. *What kind of mother are you, breaking a promise to Lesa?* it scoffed at me. *You told her you'd go with her. Now here you sit, shuffling your papers and sending her away like she was some kind of annoyance to you.*

I had done it again. Despite the good advice I'd received from others and despite the lessons I'd learned through my own previous experiences, I'd failed again. I had made office work more important than keeping a promise to my child.

When enlightenment finally struck, I wanted with all my heart to call Lesa and say, "Wait! I'm coming. I wasn't thinking. Of course I'll go with you. I said I would—and I will."

But this happened in the days before cell phones, so I *couldn't* call her back. Instead, I called God. "Oh, Father! Give me another chance. Bring her back to me, and let me start over," I prayed.

And wouldn't you know? A few minutes later, Lesa walked back through my door. She'd forgotten her sunglasses and had to return for them.

"Thank you, Jesus!" I cried when I saw her.

"Is something wrong, Mama?" she asked, alarmed by my high-volume greeting.

"Yes, something's wrong," I answered. "I got my priorities out of whack. You are much more important to me than any piece of paper could ever be, Lesa, but just for a moment I forgot that fact. I prayed that God would bring you back to me so we could go together—and he did."

Lesa's smile that day is something I can still see in my memory. Thank goodness *that* image always accompanies those pesky mental mutterings that bring my repeated failures to mind in the first place. And most importantly, thank God that he uses our mistakes to make us better. He uses "the stone that the builders rejected" (the unlikely, the misfit, the flawed, the failure) and makes it his "chief cornerstone" (the role model, the leader, the mentor). That's you and me, honey! In this life, we'll always be imperfect. But, through God's good grace and glory, he uses us anyway! He uses our mistakes, even when we make the same ones over and over.

So, sister, whenever you've done something stupid—whenever you've made a mistake that makes you feel like a failure—ask the Builder of the universe to use that failure for the good of his kingdom. Ask him to give you a second chance so you can stop being a reject and, instead, become something both you and God can rejoice about.

The Long Road from Failure to Success

Now, just because God's going to use your failures to help you make improvements in your life, that doesn't mean it's always going to happen quickly—or easily. A few verses *before* that "chief cornerstone" passage in Psalm 118, the psalmist wrote, "The Lord has chastened me severely" (v. 18).

Have you ever been "chastened" for a mistake you've made? I've had quite a few of those experiences, and they started early in my life. They weren't pleasant, but I learned from every one of them. I learned an invaluable lesson from a mistake I made as a teenager, working one summer for an apartment-rental agency in Dallas owned by a man named Mr. Ford.

It was very common for Mr. Ford's tenants to come into the office to pay their rent with cash, and one day Mr. Ford left me alone in the office while everyone else was out. I was totally in charge, he told me, and he left a rather large amount of cash—the change fund—so I could make change for those who didn't have the exact amount.

One tenant came in to pay his rent, and I gave him back too much money as change. Way too much. I didn't count out his change carefully. I guess I was nervous, having what seemed at the time to be a huge responsibility for a teenage girl. I made a mistake. When Mr. Ford came back into the office and checked his money, the amount wasn't right. I had given the tenant back too much in change.

Mr. Ford told me, "I know you didn't do this deliberately. But there has to be consequences for what you've done."

Mr. Ford was a successful businessman who could easily afford to take money out of his own pocket to correct the change fund. But he wanted me to learn a lesson—two of them, in fact. He said, "When you're dealing with money, you have to be very careful. You have to be alert and watch what you're doing."

That was lesson number one. I never again let my nervousness or a tenant's impatience keep me from counting and recounting money when I was involved in a business transaction. I took a breath and focused on what I was doing. And, remember, I went on to make a career in banking, where counting big amounts of money was an everyday task. So that was a valuable lesson, indeed.

The second lesson came from the way Mr. Ford handled my mistake. He was a wealthy man. He could have said, "Ah, that's OK, cutie-pie. You're just a dumb girl, so of course you're gonna make mistakes. I'll take care of it."

Instead, Mr. Ford expected the best of me, and he wanted me to learn from my mistake. Maybe he saw back then that although I seemed like an unlikely candidate, I had "chief cornerstone" possibilities. He told me, "The only way I can emphasize this lesson to you is to make you pay me back the amount of money you mistakenly gave away. You don't have to pay it back all at once. I'll take a little out of your paycheck every week and put it in the change fund until you've made up the difference."

In handling things that way, Mr. Ford prolonged the already difficult lesson for me—and helped me relearn it again every week when my paycheck was short. He also helped me see that mistakes can produce unpleasant consequences, but they can also be valuable learning experiences.

Sometimes we can't see what we're learning from a failure. Sometimes a mistake doesn't seem like a failure as much as it seems unfair. Those are the times when we whine, "I did what I was supposed to, so why didn't things work out the way they were supposed to?" Only later, sometimes much later, do we see how that failure was really part of God's plan to improve and prepare us.

After I left the banking industry as an employee, I started my own banking-related speaking and instructional business. For a few years everything went well, and I got smarter and smarter about banking. Girlfriend, I knew so much about banking I was a walking encyclopedia! The problem was, that encyclopedia only covered one topic. So when the banking business failed back in the eighties, I failed too. Banking was the only thing I knew how to do.

I started looking around for some other work, and one of the things I tried was writing proposals for government contracts. It was awful. I thought I knew what I was doing, but guess what: I was wrong. The truth was, I was scared, afraid I would make a mistake in writing the proposals and I would lose the contracts. I spent nearly a year writing proposals, trying to get those contracts to set up training programs, and I also tried to line up thirty to forty people to help me fulfill the contracts if I got them. That wasn't easy either.

The proposals had to be written a certain way with the

various elements organized along specific guidelines. One of the clients I would be serving if I got the contracts had been through the process before. He said, "Write the proposal this way, and I guarantee you'll get it."

Well, I shifted things around, and I wrote the proposals the way he suggested, and guess what: he was wrong too. I didn't get the contracts, and I was hurt and scared, because I was getting desperate for money. The truth was, Ms. Hotsy-Totsy Know-It-All Thelma Wells was flat broke. Talk about a failure! I was six nickels short of a quarter.

When I called to ask why I didn't get the contract, I was told that the whole program had been squashed, so the component I wanted to contract for wasn't needed. That's what I was told, but I couldn't stop thinking that if my proposals had been better written, if they had outlined a better system, presented a more confident image, expressed a better idea, then the program would have continued and I would have gotten those contracts.

That's when I started the whiny-why prayers: *God, why? Why did you let this happen to me? Why did you squash that project, Lord? Why couldn't you let me do this?*

What a mess I was—financially and emotionally and even hormonally. My life went into a tailspin as my emotions and hormones seized full control of my feelings and my reactions to all that stress. I ranted and raved and fussed and fumed. And now, looking back, I can see the truth of what Marilyn Meberg says today: emotions don't have brains. To which I've added the Thelma Wells corollary: and hormones don't have good sense.

To my surprise, though, life went on, the world kept turning, God didn't fall off his throne, and gradually I realized the truth that he knew what he was doing. Imagine that! It finally dawned on me that I hadn't been ready to fulfill the kind of government contracts I'd been trying to get. I started thinking about what would have happened if I had gotten those contracts when I didn't even have a bookkeeper or an accountant to keep track of the money, and I felt like I'd had a near miss with a head-on train. I had no idea how to do payroll or withhold taxes or any of that stuff. Can you picture the mess I would have landed in by sending out thirty people, including some I barely knew, to do training when I had no system in place to keep track of them or hold them accountable? Girlfriend, if I had gotten that contract, I'd probably be writing this book today from the poorhouse—if not federal prison!

I look back on that unanswered prayer, and I say, "God, thank you! Thank you for knowing what I need and don't need and when I'm ready for the next step. You knew that writing those proposals would give me time and training to prepare for the next step—and that next step *wasn't* fulfilling those contracts! Thank you for letting me fail, Lord."

You see, simply *writing* the proposals gave me the discipline to write in a specified way. The experience also gave me the insight I needed to recognize my mission and my vision, to pull together my credentials, to see who I really am and what I really want to do. It was an exercise in identity.

Listen up, honey. God is in control. As Sheila Walsh reminds her Women of Faith audiences, he's in control of our careers, our relationships, our finances, our marriages, our children, our churches, our communities, our state, our nation—our everything! It's only when *we* try to take control that things get messed up—and for me that's just about every doggone day.

I wanted those contracts. I worked my heart out writing those proposals. When I failed to get what I was striving for, I thought I had failed. For years I couldn't see that my "failure" had actually prepared me for what was coming next.

And what *was* coming?

I got an opportunity to speak for an organization called

Career Track preparing all-day seminars based on the career-enhancement materials they gave me to present, intertwined with my own life stories. The material had to be arranged according to specific guidelines, and the presentations had to be made a certain way. When you plan a day-long seminar, there's an order, a discipline, that must be followed, and what do you know? After a year of writing contract proposals, I found myself a lot more disciplined and sequence oriented than I'd been in the past. I did well with Career Track, and that job opened up other opportunities that carried me forward into a new, successful future.

Now let's fast-forward twenty years or more. I'm now writing proposals again, proposals related to goals I've set for my mentoring program, Daughters of Zion, as well as for books I'm planning to write. So that "failure" back in the mideighties is still providing me with the means to achieve success all these years later.

I didn't even think about how the two were connected until that morning at a Women of Faith conference when Sheila pointed out what I already knew—that God is in control of *everything*. Then, *ding!* The memory of that past, unpleasant experience popped into my mind, and along with it came the realization that I was in the midst of writing proposals and seeking grants and other financial support for the goals I'm striving for today. I'm not afraid to write a proposal now. I know how to pull things together and follow strict guidelines. Sometimes now I write a proposal in a day—and believe it or not, I enjoy doing it.

You see, this time I'm prepared. I know what I'm getting into. I have expertise in the endeavor I'm proposing, and I also have experts on hand to help me fulfill the work I'm seeking.

Yes! God knew in the 1980s what I would need in the 2000s, and he helped me lay the foundation for the success I'm enjoying now. God's plan has brought me to where I am today, and there's no telling where it will take me. Girl, when God tells us he can make everything work for good, believe it! I'm enjoying a successful, widely varied career today, and the best part of it is this: *it all began from a failure.*

Can you see why I'm tellin' you there's *no such thing* as failure? You may cease to do what you "proposed" to do. You may have a setback that wipes you out financially, physically, and emotionally. Maybe that's where you are right now. But hang in there, honey! I've been wiped out in all those ways, but here I am today, still standing on God's promises, still passing them on to you. God is in control. He takes what seems to be a failure and creates success for us when we study his Word, connect with him in prayer, and follow his ways.

God Fulfills His Gracious Promises

In the Old Testament book of Jeremiah, there's a story about a massive failure that resulted in the people of Israel being exiled from Jerusalem to Babylon. Now, living in Babylon wasn't what they had planned for themselves. It wasn't where they had expected to live out their lives, rear their children, and find fulfilling work. But that's where they ended up. And here's what God said to them through the prophet Jeremiah while they were there, stuck in the middle of that failure:

> "Build houses and settle down; plant gardens and eat what they produce. Marry and have sons and daughters; find wives for your sons and give your daughters in marriage, so that they too may have sons and daughters. Increase in number there; do not decrease. Also, seek the peace and prosperity of the city to which I have carried you into exile. Pray to the LORD for it, because if it prospers, you too will prosper." . . .
>
> "When seventy years are completed for Babylon, I

will come to you and fulfill my gracious promise to bring you back to this place. For I know the plans I have for you," declares the LORD, "plans to prosper you and not to harm you, plans to give you hope and a future. Then you will call upon me and come and pray to me, and I will listen to you. You will seek me and find me when you seek me with all your heart. I will be found by you," declares the LORD, "and will bring you back from captivity. I will gather you from all the nations and places where I have banished you," declares the LORD, "and will bring you back to the place from which I carried you into exile." (Jeremiah 29:4–7, 10–14 NIV)

God saw that the people of Israel were in a hard place; he knew they were suffering through a failure. He told them to be patient, to endure, to go about their lives, and most importantly, to continue believing in him and in his promises to them. He had a plan for them, he said, a plan that would change their failure into prosperity. He urged them to pray, to listen, to seek him out in the midst of their distress.

And, sister, that's what he's tellin' you and me today.

The Blessings of a
Messy Life

It was good for me to be afflicted
so that I might learn your decrees.
The law from your mouth is more precious to me
than thousands of pieces of silver and gold.
—Psalm 119:71–72 niv

My house isn't really anything special to look at. It's not a fabulous, new showplace sitting high on a hill in suburbia. In the inner city near downtown Dallas, it's one of a handful of custom-built homes from the 1950s that comprise a small, quiet subdivision.

No, it's not a fancy place, but I love it. It's a place where all my children and grandchildren can come with friends and other family members and feel at ease. When they come, they have the run of the house; there is no room that's off limits to them. There is no chair they cannot sit in (except Papa's green La-Z-Boy, and as I told you earlier, the little granddaughters do push the envelope on that rule now and then, just to hear Papa teasingly holler at them). My grandchildren and great-grandchildren run around the house singing, playing church, arranging talent shows, dancing, creating artful masterpieces to go on my refrigerator, teasing each other, and asking Papa if they can have a box of juice out of the little refrigerator he bought just so they could help themselves.

I love having my boisterous family together in my home, but there is a price to pay for that pleasure. At almost any time of day on any day of the week, I can look around my house and see fingerprints on the etched-glass windows and doors, faded pencil or crayon marks on a wall that one of the parents has tried to clean up, forgotten toys peeking out from under the edge of the beds, scarves and other accessories hanging out of my chest of drawers from the grandkids playing dress-up, juice spots on the rug (despite a monthly visit from my friendly neighborhood carpet-cleaning service), and dried smudges of jelly on the kitchen counter. I see these things, and I have a choice. I can sigh and fret and complain that those darn kids have messed up my house again, or I can smile and remember the fun we had, the joy we shared, and the love that filled every molecule of air while they were here.

I don't have to tell you which of those attitudes I choose, do I?

Now, I like a clean home as much as anyone, and one of the lessons Granny drilled into my head repeatedly was the old adage that cleanliness is next to godliness. There are some things I have to have really CLEAN. I can hardly eat a baked potato these days without wishing I had a magnifying glass to look for dirt on the skin—the legacy of being raised by someone who scrubbed her potatoes with a Brillo pad. And I'm trying to train my grandchildren to pick up after themselves and leave a room the way they found it. But to tell the truth, I'll probably never win an award from the folks at *Good Housekeeping* or *Better Homes and Gardens*. That's OK. I don't need another dust-catcher! And to be honest, I hope I never hear one of my grandchildren tell a friend, "My Grammy is the *best* housekeeper. You could eat off her floors, and there's not one thing out of place in her entire home."

That's not how I want to be remembered by my grandchildren. I want them to think of Grammy and Papa's house as a place where wonderful memories were created; I want them to think of fun times, welcoming gestures, nurturing embraces, comfortable reassurance, and un-conditional love. I want them to think of my house and smile, remembering a place they always want to come to. In that regard, I share a sentiment with former president George Bush, whose statement about family is inscribed on a wall in his presidential library at Texas A&M University in College Station: "What am I proudest of? The fact that my children still come home."

Now, girlfriend, you and I both know there are pros and cons to that statement. Most of us probably hope our children will always want to come home. But we also hope they'll leave! Believe me, as a parent whose children live within a fifteen-minute drive of my house, there are times when their departures bring me as much joy as their frequent arrivals! But even as I stand in the door, waving good-bye, exhausted and eagerly looking forward to a nice, quiet, solitary bubble bath, I call to them, "Y'all come back. I'll see ya soon. Call me."

Godly Relationships

I want my kids and grandkids to always feel drawn to "still come home," even if they sometimes create a mess of biblical proportions! Now, I know some of you are fastidious housekeepers, and a tidy house where nothing is ever out of place and the only thing showing on your living room carpet is sweeper tracks may be just your cup of tea. But I would encourage you to loosen up a little whenever you get an opportunity to host a gathering of family or friends. Put the breakables away if you're worried they'll get damaged. Then have fun.

And when your guests go home, walk through your messed-up house and let yourself be reminded of the loved ones who've been there. As you wash dishes or put things away, think of those who used them. Recall the echo of their laughter, the memory of your conversations, the comfort of mutually nurturing love, or maybe even the tears of condolence that rolled down your cheeks. Life's ups and downs are meant to be shared. In Jesus's parable of the shepherd who finds his lost sheep, we're told that after the shepherd finds the wandering lamb, he goes home and "calls together his friends and neighbors, saying to them, 'Rejoice with me'" (Luke 15:6).

God created us as social beings, and remember: he created us in his image (see Genesis 1:27). Throughout Scripture we see that he longs to have us communicate with him and stay spiritually close to him. In Jeremiah 29:12 God said, "Then you will call upon Me and go and pray to Me, and I will listen to you," and the apostle James urged us to "draw near to God and He will draw near to you" (James 4:8). The way I see it, if we're created in his image and he wants to nurture a strong relationship with us, then he must expect us to also have strong relationships with those who are dearest to us here on earth. He wants us to get together with one another, and he promises to be with us in our godly gatherings. Jesus said, "Where two or three are gathered together in My name, I am there in the midst of them" (Matthew 18:20).

Relax and Enjoy the Mess

Filling your home with family and friends to rejoice together, eat together, or grieve together can be a messy experience. But the payoff is worth it, as taught by the little two-line lesson in Proverbs 14:4: "An empty stable stays clean, but no income comes from an empty stable" (NLT). The New American Standard Bible puts it this way: "Where no oxen are, the manger is clean, but much revenue comes by the strength of the ox."

You see, even in biblical times, successful farmers liked to keep their barns clean, and the very easiest way to keep them clean would have been to not have any live-stock at all. Think of those huge oxen, trackin' in mud and makin' stinky messes. But without the oxen, how could the farmer till his fields, transport his produce to market, provide meat and milk for his family, and generate income by selling the surplus animals as his herd grew in number? A farmer without oxen was also without wealth.

The same principle applies to my life today. I probably could keep my home spotlessly clean if that wild Wells-family whirlwind didn't blast through my doors two or three times a month. But just think how much poorer I would be in joy, love, and laughter while I was living in that picture-perfect home.

Which choice are you making—an empty, clean "barn" or the messy wealth of owning "oxen"? Listen up, honey. A little messiness is what makes your life matter; it gives your family history more color and more meaning. Imagine getting to be an old woman (or man) without ever having to face hardships or endure difficulties. How could you really understand what it feels like to triumph over adversity if you'd always succeeded and never failed? How could you believe Jesus's statement that it's "more blessed to give than to receive" (Acts 20:35) if everything's always been handed to you? How could you know what it means to really trust someone if you'd never been betrayed? How could you appreciate God's amazing gift of grace if you'd never had to ask his forgiveness for making some kind of horrendous, hurtful, and hopelessly stupid mistake?

I know a woman who has gone through some rough times. Honey, I'm talkin' *really* rough times. Yet her faith is strong, and her attitude is joyful. One of her small pleasures is watching the sun go down in the evening. She calls herself a connoisseur of sunsets, and she has made this observation: a sunset—and a life—are richer, deeper, and more vibrant when there are clouds.

A sun that sets cleanly, without clouds, turns the sky a soft, pretty pink. That kind of sunset is OK but nothing special. In contrast, when there's a messy sky with patches of dark clouds hovering over the horizon to reflect back the full, glorious colors of the sunset, then the sky is streaked with a magnificent spectrum of incredible hues: deep purple, hot pink, velvety gray, flashing crimson, vivid violet, and dozens of other colors. That kind of sunset takes your breath away.

Sister, when I tell you that hard times and messy relationships can help you appreciate your blessings later on, you'd better believe me! Most people who know me today will tell you I am a happy, joyful person, but I've known some hard, hard times.

Granny Harrell raised me in a humble back-alley apartment, but it was a palace compared with the place my young, disabled mother lived. When I visited her in the small tent she had set up on a vacant lot, we slept together on a narrow cot.

Granny's husband, Daddy Harrell, babysat me while Granny worked as a domestic for an aristocratic family. Whenever Daddy Harrell couldn't watch me for some reason, I was sent to the home of another relative who locked me in a dark, narrow coat closet all day, saying that was the only way she could make sure I was safe.

Hard times, for sure.

I know what it's like to watch a movie from the "colored section" up in the balcony. I've waited at the back door of restaurants, out by the garbage cans, to buy a hamburger from businesses that wouldn't serve black people in the dining area. I attended segregated elementary and high schools, was denied a spot in a business school because of my race, and during college lived with four other African-American girls in a cubbyhole space in the dormitory basement next to the boiler room. It was the only dorm room the university's black female students were allowed to occupy.

I've endured a broken heart, an empty bank account, and a serious health problem more times than I care to remember. But all those messes in my past—and those I may face in my future—just serve as the dark canvas that makes the bright happiness of my life today all the more noticeable, all the more precious.

You know, Jesus told us we would have trouble in this world (see John 16:33), and honey, he wasn't kidding! But he also said he would be with us through our troubles and bring us to a glorious reward. Repeatedly, he has already helped me turn my troubles into joy so that today my life is full and happy—and I'm still living here on old planet Earth. Just imagine what kind of happiness he has in store for me when I move on to that grand family gathering up in heaven!

The same is true of life. The messy mixture of sunshine and sorrow, happiness and heartache, triumph and tragedy, rest and toil is not the easiest recipe for a full, vibrant life. But it *is* the recipe. We need to be able to look back on our past and appreciate our successes *and* our failures. We need to recognize God's presence beside us every step of the way, leading us through the good times, guiding us through the hard times, and carrying us through those times when we couldn't make it on our own. The fun we've had, the mistakes we've made, the smudges that have kept us from having a spotlessly clean past, the way others have touched our lives and left an impact, good or bad—those are the "messes" left by the "oxen" that have enriched our lives. We need good stories to tell, girlfriend! We need to have learned some lessons the hard way so when we pass those lessons on to others, we'll have the experience to back up what we're teaching.

Don't hold back from living an active, outwardly focused life because you're afraid you might make a mess of things. Don't sit home alone in your immaculate house and worry that a guest might carry in a particle of dust. Remember that *you* are dust! Sure, dust can be disturbing when it's just dust. But add a few other ingredients, and dust can become so much more: a road leading you to others, a sculpture that inspires, a shelter when you need rest, a source of children's laughter when they're playing in the mud.

Go out there and make some messes, girlfriend. Let the Living Water of our Lord Jesus Christ flow into your dusty soul, then have fun stirring up some marvelous spiritual mud pies. Celebrate the blessings of your messy life!

OTHER SELECTIONS FOR WOMEN OF FAITH

Best-Selling authors and Women of Faith® speakers Patsy Clairmont, Mary Graham, Barbara Johnson, Marilyn Meberg, Grammy Award Winning singer Sandi Patty, Luci Swindoll, Sheila Walsh, Thelma Wells and dramatist Nicole Johnson bring humor and insight to women's daily lives. Sit back, exhale, and enjoy spending some time with these extraordinary women!

WOMEN OF FAITH®
contagious JOY 2006

2006 EVENT CITIES & SPECIAL GUESTS

FEBRUARY 23-25
NATIONAL
FT. LAUDERDALE, FL
BankAtlantic Center

MARCH 31-APRIL 1
SHREVEPORT, LA
CenturyTel Center
*Avalon, Kathy Troccoli,
Anita Renfroe,
Donna VanLiere*

APRIL 7-8
HOUSTON, TX
Toyota Center
*Avalon, Max Lucado,
Chonda Pierce,
Donna VanLiere*

APRIL 21-22
SPOKANE, WA
Spokane Arena
*Avalon, Natalie Grant,
Anita Renfroe*

APRIL 28-29
COLUMBUS, OH
Nationwide Arena
*Natalie Grant,
Anita Renfroe,
Jennifer Rothschild*

JUNE 2-3
OMAHA, NE
Qwest Center
*Avalon, Anita Renfroe,
Tammy Trent,
Donna VanLiere*

JUNE 9-10
ROCHESTER, NY
Blue Cross Arena
*Avalon, Kathy Troccoli,
CeCe Winans,
Donna VanLiere*

JUNE 16-17
FRESNO, CA
SaveMart Center*
*Avalon, Natalie Grant,
Max Lucado,
Donna VanLiere*

JUNE 23-24
ATLANTA, GA
Philips Arena
*Avalon,
Nichole Nordeman,
Sherri Shepherd,
Donna VanLiere*

JULY 7-8
CHICAGO, IL
United Center
*Avalon,
Anita Renfroe,
CeCe Winans*

JULY 14-15
CLEVELAND, OH
Quicken Loans Arena
*Avalon, Natalie Grant,
Sherri Shepherd*

JULY 21-22
WASHINGTON, DC
MCI Center
*Avalon, Chonda Pierce,
Sherri Shepherd*

JULY 28-29
CALGARY, ALBERTA
Pengrowth Saddledome*
*Avalon, Carried Away,
Max Lucado,
Donna VanLiere*

AUGUST 4-5
ST. LOUIS, MO
Savvis Center
*Natalie Grant,
Anita Renfroe,
Sherri Shepherd,
Donna VanLiere*

AUGUST 11-12
HARTFORD, CT
Hartford Civic Center
*Avalon, Carol Kent,
Jennifer Rothschild*

AUGUST 18-19
FT. WAYNE, IN
War Memorial Coliseum
*Avalon, Natalie Grant,
Carol Kent*

AUGUST 25-26
DALLAS, TX
American Airlines Center
*Max Lucado,
Natalie Grant,
Robin McGraw*

SEPTEMBER 8-9
ANAHEIM, CA
Arrowhead Pond
*Avalon, Robin McGraw,
Jennifer Rothschild*

SEPTEMBER 15-16
PHILADELPHIA, PA
Wachovia Center
*Avalon, Robin McGraw,
Nicole C. Mullen*

SEPTEMBER 22-23
DENVER, CO
Pepsi Center
*Max Lucado,
Chonda Pierce,
Kathy Troccoli*

SEPTEMBER 29-30
SACRAMENTO, CA
ARCO Arena
*Avalon, Robin McGraw,
Nichole Nordeman*

OCTOBER 6-7
OKLAHOMA CITY,
Ford Center
*Avalon, Max Lucado,
Jennifer Rothschild,
Donna VanLiere*

OCTOBER 13-14
PORTLAND, OR
Rose Garden Arena
*Avalon, Carol Kent,
Kathy Troccoli,
Donna VanLiere*

OCTOBER 20-21
ST. PAUL, MN
Xcel Energy Center
*Avalon, Carol Kent,
Anita Renfroe*

OCTOBER 27-28
CHARLOTTE, NC
Charlotte Arena
*Avalon, Chonda Pierce,
Jennifer Rothschild*

NOVEMBER 3-4
VANCOUVER, BC
GM Place*
*Avalon, Carried Away,
Nichole Nordeman,
Donna VanLiere*

NOVEMBER 10-11
ORLANDO, FL
TD Waterhouse Center
*Avalon,
Nicole C. Mullen,
Anita Renfroe,
Donna VanLiere*

NOVEMBER 17-18
PHOENIX, AZ
Glendale Arena*
*Avalon,
Nichole Nordeman,
Kathy Troccoli,
Donna VanLiere*

1-888-49-FAITH womenoffaith.com

*No Pre-Conference available. Dates, times, locations and special guests subject to change.
Visit womenoffaith.com for details on special guests, registration deadlines and pricing.